Urban Decision Making

A GUIDE TO INFORMATION SOURCES

Volume 13 in the Urban Studies Information Guide Series

Mark L. Drucker

*Director of the Graduate Urban Affairs
and Policy Analysis Program
Southern Illinois University of Edwardsville*

Gale Research Company
Book Tower, Detroit, Michigan 48226

Library of Congress Cataloging in Publication Data

Drucker, Mark L
    Urban decision making.

    (Urban studies information guide series ; v. 13)
(Gale information guide library)
    Includes index.
    1. City planning—Decision making—Bibliography.
2. Urban policy—Decision making—Bibliography.
I. Title. II. Series.
Z5942.D77 [HT166] 016.352'0004725 80-19252
ISBN 0-8103-1481-9

VITA

Mark L. Drucker is director of the graduate urban affairs and policy analysis program at Southern Illinois University of Edwardsville. His course assignments include laboratories in issue analysis, in strategic budget planning, and in program design and evaluation, as well as courses in management. He received his B.A. in 1969 with a major in urban studies-government from Columbia College, Columbia University, and M.B.A. in 1971 from Harvard Graduate School of Business Administration.

Drucker is consultant to the Danforth Foundation, evaluating the St. Louis Leadership Program. He is a member of the plan development committee, Greater St. Louis Health Systems Agency; board of directors, Metro Housing Resources; steering committee, Harvard Business School Club; and chairman for the St. Louis Secondary School Committee for Columbia College. He was a 1974 recipient of the Dean's Award from Columbia College, Columbia University.

CONTENTS

ACKNOWLEDGMENTS

It would not have been possible to complete this work, were it not for the co-operation of a great many individuals and agencies. First and foremost, I appreciate the help of all the individuals and agencies who were nice enough to mail me copies of their materials. Alfred Kahn, Michael Quinn, and Clyde Bishop, who have administered the urban programs at Southern Illinois University at Edwardsville over the last two years, made the time available to me to do this work. Thomas Murphy, the editor of this series, was a source of enthusiastic support. Marvin Soloman and other staff members of SIU-E's Lovejoy Library helped a great deal by ordering a significant number of hardbound books for me for Lovejoy's collections. Dolores Kohler, Paula White, Sue Tognarelli, and Rose Modene were generous in their assistance in typing both the manuscript and the correspondence required to complete the project. Vincent Aquilino, my graduate assistant, was a valuable source of help in searching for the most appropriate materials. Also very much appreciated was the editorial help of the Gale Information Guide Series staff--Denise Allard Adzigian, Pamela Dear, and Donna Batten.

Many of the bibliographic reference sources in this field provided me with useful starts in the review of different aspects of the literature. Most fundamentally of all, my colleagues in the urban policy analysis profession provided me with the intellectual framework upon which the organization of this annotated bibliography is based.

INTRODUCTION

The annotated bibliography which I have compiled has a special purpose. It is designed to make accessible to a wider audience a great deal of the work which those of us in the urban policy analysis profession have been doing over the last seventeen years. The literature which has been listed and described demonstrates the urban policy analysis methods which have been and are presently being utilized for decision-making purposes in public and nonprofit agencies throughout the United States.

These books, articles, monographs, case studies, and reports have been assembled and reviewed manually through the cooperation and thoughtfulness of innumerable academics and practitioners. Computerized data retrieval systems will hopefully supplant individual efforts of this sort in the future. At this point, the literature is far too diffuse and insufficiently systematically organized to allow for assistance of this kind. It is hoped that this bibliography might help professional education faculty members in their curriculum development efforts and agency professionals in their staff training functions. If it does prove useful in these ways, it will be as a result of its particular organization and array of materials in juxtaposition to one another.

The work which follows was initiated in the fall of 1971, when a new graduate professional education model in urban policy analysis was developed at the New School for Social Research in New York City. At that time this author was asked to play a modest role in the development of that process by Jack Ukeles, then the department's new chairman, and more recently executive director of New York City's Management Advisory Board. That department was founded with the purpose of translating the best work in urban policy analysis practice into tangible graduate professional education preparation for careers in America's cities. From the outset, those who were to teach in that program relied extensively upon the high standards and traditions of the professionals drafting the strategic plans, constructing the budgets, designing and evaluating the programs, and analyzing the bases for the decisions confronting American cities.

This annotated bibliography is designed to highlight that body of work and the work which followed. It was both the observational and the synthesizing skills of Jack Ukeles which made the idea of such a curriculum viable. His decision to organize the curriculum around four specific key decision-making roles is the basis for the outline of this annotated bibliography. In the late 1970s, there continues to be a need for the rigorous analytic preparation of professionals who will perform these roles. While the graduate urban affairs and policy analysis program at Southern Illinois University of Edwardsville presently chooses to organize its curriculum in this way, it is hoped that other academic institutions and training processes might also come to select some of these approaches for their own use.

The message of this work is that there are significant commonalities in the analysis being undertaken in a wide variety of different settings in American cities and state, regional, and federal agencies.

Schools of business and public administration, urban planning, urban studies, policy analysis, social work and social policy, health administration, educational administration, criminal justice, and systems analysis are all represented. Students in each discipline too rarely glimpse the similar analytic thinking of their colleagues in other disciplines.

All of the fields of urban service delivery are represented: housing, economic development, criminal justice, health; social services; manpower, transportation, environmental protection, and education. It is no secret that practitioners in each field have difficulty in keeping current with much of the literature developed in other fields.

There is a sampling of literature from a variety of different institutional sources in the urban environment: traditional and highly applied academic policy research centers; governmental research groups; public agencies at all levels of government; voluntary organizations; corporate social action offices; community action agencies; private consulting firms; and advocacy organizations articulating urban needs. My own work several years ago in cataloging for the first time the analytic products of university urban centers illustrated how totally ill-equipped even the most collegial of these institutions were in knowing the work of their counterparts in other parts of the country.

Yet there are common needs for methodologic skills for urban decision making which cut across these boundaries. "Demand" in nonprofit marketing and "needs analysis" in planning can be viewed as complementary skills. "Objective-setting" and "issue analysis" need not be viewed as contradictory approaches, despite the differences in the bases for their origination respectively in private and public enterprise settings. Planners and policy analysts can offer budgeters a strategic framework for establishing priorities in resource allocation. The work which follows will attempt to explore some of these analytic commonalities.

In a simple introductory manner, this annotated bibliography proposes to lay out choices which can lead to synthesis and broader conceptual cohesiveness. The reader is likely to encounter familiar sources, discussed in unconventional ways, and other sources, highlighted for reasons highly specific to the objectives of this undertaking. No insult is intended to the more basic concerns of the authors of each work. It is hoped instead that sound analysis in many cases may be employed profitably in somewhat new ways.

Naturally limited by not possessing all of the skills of either a social scientist or a quantitative methodologist, I have selected far too little of the work representative of these fields. Full curriculum concepts teaching decision making for basic urban policy analysis roles should build extensively upon those literatures for both context and illustrative examples. Other volumes in this series are likely to help contribute to that purpose. In this volume, there is a presentation of qualitative analysis needed to perform the issue analysis urban decision-making role specifically.

Walt Kelly wrote in "Pogo" that "we are all confronted with insurmountable opportunities." It is for the purpose of helping urban policy analysts succeed in a little bit of "surmounting" that this annotated bibliography on urban decision-making analytic processes has been compiled.

ISSUE ANALYSIS AS A BASIC TECHNIQUE OF
URBAN DECISION MAKING

The proponents of Planning Programming Budgeting Systems (PPBS) reforms in the 1960s may have deserved better, but it seems likely that their longest standing impact may be measured in the revolutionary effect they had upon the basic executive decision-making memorandum.

Government executives in the 1970s are often inclined to take pride in the length of their agendas of policy issues which require decisions. In particular, an activist decision maker might choose to self-consciously hold on to his/her opportunities to intervene in a variety of different areas of social policy. A decision maker with a more selective view of his/her potential for effective action is likely, nevertheless, to be reminded of outstanding policy issues by an increasingly well-educated press corps, trained to focus on the more substantive aspects of public policy.

Confronted with a wide range of diverse policy issues, often involving specialized technical content, decision makers have frequently come to require of their staff members lucid summarized statements of the alternative ways in which issues might be resolved. PPBS provided a format for these statements—the issue paper—and increasingly analysis of this kind has come to dominate the internal memoranda that decision makers choose to review.

More significantly, PPBS provided the impetus for popularizing the addition of the next step past the issue paper—the program analysis—to the decision-making process. Program analysis, in turn, has been adapted into issue analysis, a somewhat more elegant technique for reviewing policy decisions involving issues as well as programs. Both approaches embody the most accessible, intuitively familiar aspects of rational analysis. An issue is defined, and alternative ways of responding are generated. Each alternative is then evaluated against the relevant criteria for an acceptable decision. The complementary analogue to issue analysis in the private sector has been decision analysis reviewing comparative investment alternatives with a decision tree format.

President Gerald Ford worked with just such documents during his term in the White House. President Carter is said to have used issue papers as governor of

Georgia, and to have institutionalized the development of similar documents within the Executive Office. In American cities, issue analysis is frequently viewed as the introductory step toward rationalizing the policymaking process, the sort of politically useful advice which wins policy analysis its first spurs with decision makers.

The significance of the use of this approach to memorandum development can best be understood by acknowledging what issue analyses do not do. Conventionally "quick and dirty" documents, on a local level, they are not particularly likely to reflect social science research findings. While they often include a preferred alternative, this alternative is more likely to look best in the trade-off analyses, rather than to appear to be the "right" answer. General theory then is not often neatly applied to a particularized case to come up with a single answer. Instead assumptions are highlighted, and limitations upon both data and causal inferences remain evident. Work on the analysis likely is concluded at the point at which a decision actually has to be made or deferred, rather than at a particularly satisfying point of intellectual mastery over the problem at hand.

The definition of objectives in the Management By Objectives (MBO) approach requires no such evaluation of and selection among alternatives. MBO, with its present widespread application in public agencies, focuses less on the selection of options and more on the subsequent managerial control of performance.

Most significantly, issue analysis allows decision makers to reflect upon the value conflicts present in a public policy decision, and the differing positions of interest groups on the issue. It is this dimension, which, when added to the assessment of potential costs and benefits, makes the process unique in its practical applicability for politically conscious public executives.

Consequently, the literature on issue analysis is organized first to highlight the method itself and examples of its application, and then around the criteria employed to evaluate alternatives: cost criteria, cost and performance criteria, and political feasibility criteria. Cost-benefit trade-offs are an important part of this process, and examples of cost-benefit literature are offered to demonstrate cost and performance criteria. The cost-benefit literature, however, has deep roots in current applied economics thinking, frequently is exemplified by very different kinds of studies, and thus will be presented in an unusually circumscribed manner in the pages which follow.

INTRODUCTION TO ISSUE ANALYSIS

Alkin, Marvin C. "Systems Analysis: Problems and Prospects." PLANNING AND CHANGING 1 (July 1970): 83-89.

>This brief article suggests to educators that rationality in decision analysis will improve their ability to exercise judgment. Issue analysis will propose not a single answer, but many reasonable alternatives. It will be more useful as a "soft" operational technique, than as a scientific research tool to predict behavior and outcomes.

Bennett, John, and Felton, Edward L., Jr. MANAGERIAL DECISION MAKING: CASE PROBLEMS IN FORMULATION AND IMPLEMENTATION. Columbus, Ohio: Grid, 1974. 187 p.

>This could easily rank as the most useful of the casebooks teaching the different elements of decision analysis. The cases cover such topics as policymaking environment; issue definition; alternatives generation; criteria development; alternatives evaluation; decision recommendation; and implementation. The cases, while all based in the private sector, address accessible business activities (beer, clothes, poultry, banking). Brief introductions to the cases discuss how to conduct each of the aspects of the analysis. There is also a teaching manual available separately.

Benton, John B. MANAGING THE ORGANIZATIONAL DECISION PROCESS. Lexington, Mass.: D.C. Heath and Co., 1973. 271 p.

>The most relevant portions of this basic text on systems planning are the chapters on issue identification, evaluation and selection of the preferred course of action, and implementation. The author describes issue identification as the proactive vehicle for organizing a policymaking process for an organization, and lays out a full effectiveness-efficiency-political feasibility matrix analysis for the review of issue alternatives. He talks about conflict, power, and bargaining as aspects of implementation approaches within a chapter reviewing some of the organizational change literature.

Black, Max, ed. PROBLEMS OF CHOICE AND DECISION. Proceedings of a colloquium held at the Aspen Institute for Humanistic Studies, 24 June-6 July 1974. Ithaca, N.Y.: Cornell University Program on Science, Technology, and Society, 1975. 828 p.

> Having prepared for the encounter by reading Howard Raiffa, fourteen humanists met at Aspen to thoroughly thrash out the philosophical troubles with rational choice. Descriptive as well as normative aspects of the theory are rousingly debated. The topic of hierarchies of preference is pursued, chiefly with normative interests in mind.

Blum, Henrick L. PLANNING FOR HEALTH: DEVELOPMENT AND APPLICATION OF SOCIAL CHANGE THEORY. New York: Human Sciences Press, 1974. 622 p.

> This is a basic conceptual approach to health systems planning. In chapter 8, the author critically reviews and adapts decision analysis as a component part of his planning system. Important caveats are noted--how procedural criteria are outweighed by social value criteria, the importance of time streams for health issues, how in evaluating alternatives weight is placed upon concepts such as "most bang for the buck," political and social acceptability, "equity," and "freedom from worry."

Burt, Marvin R. POLICY ANALYSIS: INTRODUCTION AND APPLICATION TO HEALTH PROGRAMS. Washington, D.C.: Information Resources Press, 1974. 136 p.

> The author presents his view of a form of issue analysis dominated by a single performance criterion, an approach influenced by economic and MBO analyses. However, his work offers good examples of multiple effectiveness measures to help broaden evaluation of that performance criterion. Three extensive cost-effectiveness cases are presented: maternal and child health care; family planning for American Indians; and emergency ambulance service. The latter case is especially well developed for pedagogic purposes.

Churchman, C. West. THE SYSTEMS APPROACH. New York: Delacorte Press, 1968. 243 p.

> Chapter 3, in which the author lays out the basic system's paradigm, is a basic reading for alternatives generation in an issue analysis. The author's "five basic considerations" are the total system's objectives, and, more specifically, the performance measures of the whole system; the system's environment; the fixed constraints; the resources of the system; the system's components (activities, goals, and performance measurements); and the system's management.

Coates, Joseph F. "What is a Public Policy Issue?" Paper presented at the Annual Meeting of the American Association for the Advancement of Science in Denver, Colorado, on 23 February 1977. 40 p.

> This staff member of the U.S. Office of Technology Assessment defines a public policy issue as a fundamental, enduring conflict among or between objectives, goals, customs, plans, activities, or stakeholders, which is not likely to be resolved in favor of any polar position in that conflict; that is, it is not a "problem" which can be solved. The author makes such practical points as that many issues are not "information driven," and searching for information may only result in delay. He describes both the actors and the process surrounding governmental review of issues.

District of Columbia. Office of Budget and Financial Management. ISSUE ANALYSIS: AN AID TO PROGRAM DECISION-MAKING IN URBAN GOVERNMENT. Washington, D.C.: November 1972. 43 p. Paperbound.

> During the first year of implementing an issue analysis effort, this budget bureau's work was influenced by the familiar need for evaluative information on program activities which budget agencies require for resource allocation decisions. The PPB-style issue papers in this compendium reflect this analytic bias. They cover the following topics: retirement financing; care of dependent children; narcotics treatment; solid waste disposal; citizen participation; and prepaid group health insurance.

Dorfman, Robert, ed. MEASURING BENEFITS OF GOVERNMENT INVESTMENTS. Paper presented at a conference held 7-9 November 1963. Washington, D.C.: Brookings Institution, 1965. 429 p.

> This is the anthology long used to summarize the basic arguments on costs and benefits in programs in most of the urban public service functional areas. Included are pieces by Ruth Mack and Sumner Myers on recreation; by Burton Weisbrod on dropouts; by Jerome Rothenberg on urban renewal; by Herbert Klarman on syphilis conrol; by Herbert Mohring on urban highway investment; and by Gary Fromm on civil aviation. In an introduction, the editor notes limitations on the quality of the alternatives generated in many of the papers.

Drake, Alvin W.; Keeney, Ralph L.; and Morse, Philip M., eds. ANALYSIS OF PUBLIC SYSTEMS. Cambridge: MIT Press, 1972. 532 p.

> The authors present a series of the systems analysis studies undertaken by organizations such as the New York City RAND Institute and McKinsey and Company for cities such as New York. A number of the studies are strong examples of the application of issue analysis: cost-benefit thinking for health planning; effectiveness criteria for air pollution programs; and airport facility

planning in Mexico City. The systems studies in other functional areas demonstrate the kind of research designs needed to produce issue analysis: fire, ambulance, and police emergency services; blood banking; airport runway usage; postal service; classroom activity assessment; higher education, water resources, and criminal justice systems planning concepts; and driver accident models. Also included is the famous essay by Ralph Keeney and Howard Raiffa, "A Critique of Formal Analysis in Public Decision Making," which argues for the adaptation of decision theory and systems techniques to the market requirements of public agencies.

Drucker, Mark L. "Issue Paper: How Might Fairview Heights' City Council Best Improve Its Ability to Focus on Policy Formation Issues?" Edwardsville: Southern Illinois University at Edwardsville, Center for Urban and Environmental Research and Services, February 1977. 11 p. Mimeo.

This paper offers an issue analysis that assesses how a small Illinois city might implement Public Administration Service recommendations urging the city council to improve its policy formation processes. Information-gathering, issue paper, and budget analysis alternatives are developed and contrasted, consistent with the governmental structure of Fairview Heights.

_____. "Recommendations to the City of Fairview Heights: Using Issue Papers to Help Make Policy." Edwardsville: Southern Illinois University at Edwardsville, Center for Urban and Environmental Research and Services, January 1977. 5 p. Mimeo.

Given a Public Administration Service recommendation to the city council of Fairview Heights, Illinois, that the council's policymaking processes be strengthened, this paper describes the advantages of an issue analysis approach. The questions proposed and answered in this paper include what does "improved policy formulation" mean?; what are the requirements of a better decisionmaking system?; what kinds of information are needed?; and how could such a system be implemented?

Duncan, W. Jack. DECISION MAKING AND SOCIAL ISSUES: A GUIDE TO ADMINISTRATIVE ACTION IN AN ENVIRONMENTAL CONTEXT. Hinsdale, Ill.: Dryden Press, 1973. 176 p.

This excellent basic text proposes the application of the decision analysis approach to a variety of environmental issues. Brief cases are detailed to test the approach on a series of different levels; examples of the generation of alternatives to satisfy environmental objectives are repeatedly presented.

Easton, Allan. DECISION MAKING: A SHORT COURSE FOR PROFESSIONALS. Seven programmed texts. New York: John Wiley and Sons, 1976.

Text 1: DECISION MAKING: AN OVERVIEW. 43 p.
Management by objectives and decision analysis are viewed as
representative respectively of optimizing and satisfying models.
Focused objectives, the author proposes, may be preferable to
objectives defined in a "muddling through" process. Cases,
quizzes, and reality tests are included in each text.

Text 5: TRANSLATE OUTCOME SCORES INTO VALUE SCORES
AND WEIGHT CRITERIA. 40 p.
From the utility valuation perspective, the author describes how
to weight different criteria in a criteria-choice matrix. Straight
and inverse ranking and ratio scales are described.

Text 7: SELECT A RULE AND COMPUTE BEST ALTERNATIVE;
MAKE A DECISION AND LIVE WITH IT. 65 p.
Described are the distance from a target profile rule; points of
superiority-equal and unequal weights rules; and the ratio rule.
The author discusses how to select a choice rule when criteria
may include major attributes, minor attributes, and variables.
A discussion is also included of when full explication may or
may not be desirable.

Georgetown University. Public Services Laboratory. State-Local Finances
Project. PLANNING PROGRAMMING BUDGETING FOR CITY, STATE, COUNTY
OBJECTIVES. Washington, D.C.: 1968.

P.P.B. NOTE 12: THE COST AND EFFECTIVENESS PAPER.
48 p.
Just as the Ukeles, Bales, and Hearn "Schema" provides the
basic source for analyzing an issue, this document is the basic
source for program analysis in a budget context. The only major
distinction is to be found in the objectives orientation of PPBS
which presupposes a "programmatic" decision. In this note, the
issue paper is developed into a full program analysis, by crys-
tallizing the issue definition into some objectives statements, and
going on to complete the criteria-choice matrix analysis. Effectiveness criteria measure potential success in securing the
objectives. Examples are provided for each component of the
analysis.

George Washington University. State-Local Finances Project. PLANNING
PROGRAMMING BUDGETING FOR CITY, STATE, COUNTY OBJECTIVES.
Washington, D.C.: 1968.

P.P.B. NOTE 11: A FIRST STEP TO ANALYSIS: THE ISSUE
PAPER. 10 p.
Issue papers are proposed as the transition step in the development of a PPB system. An issue paper should define the problem
and lay out the alternatives and criteria, as preparation for full
issue or program analysis. Ten elements are listed to be included in an issue paper.

Groner, Gabriel F.; Palley, Norman A.; Rockwell, Marshall A.; and Stewart, David H. APPLICATIONS OF COMPUTERS IN HEALTH CARE DELIVERY: AN OVERVIEW AND RESEARCH AGENDA. Paper 5185. Santa Monica, Calif.: Rand Corp., February 1974. 50 p.

> This paper details the computer technology aids used in auto-
> mating aspects of the clinical diagnosis process. Progress has
> been made, based on introspective analysis of clinical judg-
> ments, formalization of observed symptom disease relationships,
> and statistical manipulation of clinical history and laboratory
> data in relation to the probability of occurrence of various
> diagnostic categories. Work focused initially on electrocardio-
> grams, blood gas analysis, drug-drug interaction programs, and
> radiation therapy. A Bayesian approach is also being imple-
> mented in many health facilities, attempting to express a pa-
> tient's diagnosis and treatment process as a series of sequential
> decisions that must be made with incomplete information.

Hammond, John S. III. "Better Decisions with Preference Theory." HARVARD BUSINESS REVIEW 45 (November-December 1967): 123-41.

> This article had a major influence in helping to popularize
> preference theory. It is also valuable as a clear introduction
> to decision analysis, using the oil well digging case study.
> The author distinguishes in analyzing this case between the two
> important subjective inputs in a business decision problem--
> judgments about probabilities of events and attitudes toward
> risks. Attitudes toward risks are shown in terms of the pref-
> erence curves of decision makers as ranging from risk-averse
> to linear to risk-prone.

Hatry, Harry; Blair, Louis; Fisk, Donald; and Kimmel, Wayne. PROGRAM ANALYSIS FOR STATE AND LOCAL GOVERNMENTS. Washington, D.C.: Urban Institute, 1976. 155 p.

> This publication provides one of the best traditional explanations
> of how to conduct issue analysis. The authors present chapters
> full of loving detail on such subjects as alternatives generation,
> cost criteria design, effectiveness criteria design, and imple-
> mentation considerations. Attached are three case studies:
> short-term care for neglected children; the use of police patrol
> cars by off-duty officers; and hard drug treatment options.

Jacquez, John A., ed. COMPUTER DIAGNOSIS AND DIAGNOSTIC METHODS. Proceedings of the Second Conference on the Diagnostic Process held at the University of Michigan. Springfield, Ill.: Charles C Thomas Publishers, 1972. 397 p.

> G. Barnett, John Baillieul, and Barbara Farquhar describe the
> testing of the diagnostic skills of house staff and medical students
> against a series of computer problems. Allen Ginsberg writes

that diagnosis can be defined as either a classification or a decision-making problem. Using a decision tree, analysis can proceed from defining the syndrome, to listing possible disease states, to listing the relevant diagnostic tests, to defining the utility structure for the particular situation. Pruning is of special importance here. T. Allen Pryor and Homer Warner describe a 1961 experiment in man-computer diagnosis of two hundred congenital heart disease cases, in which only one doctor performed as well as the computer. Other articles describe more cooperative ventures.

Keeney, Ralph L., and Raiffa, Howard. DECISIONS WITH MULTIPLE OBJECTIVES: PREFERENCES AND VALUE TRADEOFFS. New York: John Wiley and Sons, 1976. 569 p.

The heart of this text on decision analysis is the authors' views on how to deal with both single attribute and multiattribute problems under both certainty and uncertainty. They present mathematical theory, as well as a series of cases on such topics as air pollution, nuclear power facilities, fire department operations, airport location, and educational and health programs.

Kraemer, Kenneth L. POLICY ANALYSIS IN LOCAL GOVERNMENT: A SYSTEMS APPROACH TO DECISIONMAKING. Washington, D.C.: International City Management Association, 1973. 165 p.

This is a practical and accessible systems analysis handbook. The author segregates urban management problems into three categories: operational; managerial or programming; and planning or developmental. A systems analysis brand of issue analysis is proposed in chapter 4, "The Process of Analysis," and a criteria-choice matrix is introduced. This work also provides a useful introduction to strategic planning concepts.

Leveson, Irving, and Weiss, Jeffrey H. ANALYSIS OF URBAN HEALTH PROBLEMS. New York: Spectrum Publications, 1976. 390 p.

This casebook is a sampler of the policy analysis projects undertaken by New York City's Health Services Administration during the Lindsay administration. Included are a mix of materials which the authors describe as: system monitoring and description pieces; program, agency, and process evaluations; methodologic and quantitative inquiries; policy development and analysis work; and program development and implementation plans. An excellent introductory chapter discusses the successes and failures of the policy analysts within the agency--influence over the design or restructuring of categorical programs and little influence over the "misallocation" of larger scale health resources(e.g., hospital closings). Among the health policies analyzed are: unnecessary hospitalization; physician staffing; tuberculosis clinics; alcoholism programs; prison health; a famous cost-benefit study of heroin addiction (by Allan Leslie); venereal disease; and home health care. Also included is the health issues transition paper prepared for Lindsay's mayoral successor.

Mack, Ruth Prince. PLANNING ON UNCERTAINTY: DECISION MAKING IN BUSINESS AND GOVERNMENT ADMINISTRATION. New York: John Wiley and Sons, 1971. 233 p.

> After an extensive review of decision analysis, concerned with the problem that uncertainty may inhibit the generation of appropriately creative alternatives, the author proposes fifty ways to cope with uncertainty. While this concluding checklist is of special interest, the decision analysis presentation is particularly clearly written, although it does not contain very many public sector examples. A case study concerning the IBM System/360 is also quite useful.

Magee, John F. "Decision Trees for Decision Making." HARVARD BUSINESS REVIEW 42 (July-August 1964): 126-38.

> This is an excellent initial reading in the fundamentals of decision analysis. Simple decision trees are presented beginning with the illustration of a cocktail party. Action and event points are presented, and gradually the basis for financial investment planning is detailed, through discussions of cash flow analysis, present value calculations, uncertainties, and end point valuation.

Mechling, Jerry E. "The Policy Analyst as Analyst, General Staff, and Change Agent: A Case Study of Program Innovation and Implementation in the New York City Environmental Protection Administration, 1968-1971." Ph.D. dissertation, Princeton University, 1974. 634 p.

> As participant observer, the author describes the need to sell the ideas generated in analysis both "up" and "down" an organization, working respectively as a general staff person (doing day-to-day work for decision makers), and as a change agent (convincing operating-level managers to employ these ideas).

Mushkin, Selma, and Herman, Brian. THE SEARCH FOR ALTERNATIVES: PROGRAM OPTIONS IN A PPB SYSTEM. Washington, D.C.: George Washington University, State-Local Finances Project, October 1968. 66 p. Paperbound.

> Program analysis is reviewed in terms of the quality of its alternatives generation processes. This paper defines possible sources as having originated from systems analysis of the problem (including a comparison of alternative levels of service); as having been developed from comparative programs, experiments, or proposals; or as having evolved as "new ideas." The relationships among research, program analysis, and idea generation are explored. A series of examples of program analyses and

alternatives developed in federal agency problem analyses are detailed in the following areas: maternal and child health care; income and benefits programs; health care for the poor; cancer; motor vehicle injury prevention; pest control; and disease control.

New York City. Mayor's Management Advisory Board. "Management Plan Revisions--Guidelines for Preparation of the FY 1978 Management Plan." New York: 22 April 1977. 61 p. Mimeo.

This manual indicates the role which issue analysis can play in an MBO-based management plan. Catalog and descriptions of critical issues are required to allow senior decision makers the opportunity to review the crucial policy decisions needed to implement the plan and manage the city's agencies.

Odiorne, George S. MANAGEMENT DECISIONS BY OBJECTIVES. Englewood Cliffs, N.J.: Prentice-Hall, 1969. 252 p.

In this work, one of the leading management by objectives theorists and proselytizers identifies his approach with issue analysis thinking. He argues for the selection of the best among alternative courses of action, and also, unlike the decision tree exponents, proposes the use of a criteria-choice matrix, focusing on feasibility as well as cost and performance criteria. Also included is a section devoted to quantitative aspects of decision-making uncertainty, probabilities, and preferences. A decision tree itself is discussed.

Quade, Edward S. ANALYSIS FOR PUBLIC DECISIONS. New York: American Elsevier Publishing Co., 1975. 336 p.

In this review of a Rand Corp. analysis, the emphasis has shifted from defense to domestic policy analysis. Included are discussions on such fundamental questions as criteria and objectives, and the limitations upon analysis.

_____. ANALYSIS FOR PUBLIC POLICY DECISIONS. Report P-4863. Santa Monica, Calif.: Rand Corp., July 1972. 25 p.

This paper, delivered in Kanagawa, Japan, is a strong and simple statement on the usefulness of rational methods for public sector problem solving. The author points out the distinctions between efficiency-oriented problems, and those problems in which political and social factors predominate. He points out that it is in the area of implementation that policy analysts have always been weakest (for example, in understanding the costs of organizational change). Clients seeking analysis should offer voluntary support for implementation, and the time needed for the work to be properly undertaken. Solutions must be within the client's capability to handle, and the client's interest must be respected. The client may need help in carrying out recommendations.

Raiffa, Howard. DECISION ANALYSIS: INTRODUCTORY LECTURES ON CHOICES UNDER UNCERTAINTY. Reading, Mass.: Addison-Wesley, 1968. 309 p.

> This is probably the best extended reference source on the use of economic system decision trees, drafted, after all, by the individual most associated with their use. Emphasis is placed upon tracking different alternatives across time, and chance events to their ultimate quantitative outcomes. Probabilities and utility values are to be employed. The author also has the wit to inquire in one of his subchapter headings: "When does a tree become a bushy mess?"

Rivlin, Alice. SYSTEMATIC THINKING FOR SOCIAL ACTION. Washington, D.C.: Brookings Institution, 1971. 150 p.

> In the 1970 H. Rowan Gaither lectures at Berkeley, the author, after dismissing issue analysis logic as common sense, presented discussions of the following topics: defining problems and who is most affected by them; the beneficiaries of possible public actions, and the extent to which they might benefit; assessing which alternative would do the most good; and assessing how to produce services most effectively. The lectures conclude with an early essay on accountability.

Rosenbloom, Richard, and Russell, John. NEW TOOLS FOR URBAN MANAGEMENT. Boston: Graduate School of Business Administration, Harvard University, 1971. 298 p.

> The authors attempt to differentiate operational analysis requirements confronted in public agencies from the elaborate systems analysis approaches common to the military. They offer interesting discussions of the problems confronted by practitioners. For example, in Dayton analysts on a manpower project work for an ineffective client under great time constraints, and make grandiose assumptions. Carter Bales's pieces on PPBS in New York and how to conduct program analysis are highlights. Bales's piece on program analysis reflects a somewhat more conventional decision analysis-oriented viewpoint than his contribution to the New School schema. However the article itself exemplifies the best standards of a good many public agencies. Mahlon Apgar's discussion of the analysis developed in the design of the Columbia new town is also valuable. In addition there are pieces about housing finance in New Jersey and firehouse site selection in East Lansing, Michigan.

Rubel, Ronald A. "Decision Analysis and Medical Diagnosis and Treatment." Ph.D. dissertation, Harvard University, 1967. 227 p.

The author applies decision analysis to three medical problems: the diagnosis of a sore throat; a diagnosis of whether a patient's high blood pressure may be caused by kidney malfunction; and a Food and Drug Administration official's decision on whether to license a new drug.

Steiss, Alan Walter. PERFORMANCE/PROGRAM BUDGETING. Policy-Program Analysis and Evaluation Techniques. Package 6, Module 6. Washington, D.C.: National Training and Development Service Urban Management Curriculum Development Project, 1977. 160 p.

Case studies focus on program analysis skills. First, the use of decision trees and probability theory is illustrated in a case involving safety improvements at five "very high hazard intersections." Next, sensitivity and contingency analyses are taught in a case concerned with the site selection process for city governmental offices. A third case lays out a problem in unit cost analysis for the maintenance of street lighting, and a fourth case study is a Los Angeles school dropout cost-effectiveness problem.

Trapp, Shel. DYNAMICS OF ORGANIZING. Chicago: National Training and Information Center, 1976. 26 p. Paperbound.

Issues, in this community organizing manual, are viewed as the fodder of antiestablishment attack and community consciousness-raising. The author proposes that a potential issue be tested for popular interest, and describes a case example of how one community could only be mobilized around the issue of "loose supermarket shopping carts."

Ukeles, Jacob B.; Bales, Carter; and Hearn, Robert. A GENERAL SCHEMA FOR ISSUE ANALYSIS. New York: New School for Social Research, Department of Urban Affairs and Policy Analysis, 1974. 31 p. Paperbound.

The New School approach broadens the issue paper and program analysis concepts into issue analysis, by employing the decision tree to array alternative responses to underlying and relaxed issues, thereby integrating more value positions into the alternatives to be analyzed. The authors propose the use of a criteria-choice matrix as the framework for evaluating the alternatives, and recommend that the analysis proceed through as many cycles as there is time to complete. This approach strongly argues for the inclusion of political feasibility, as well as cost and performance criteria.

Yearwood, Richard M. ISSUE PAPER TECHNIQUES. Policy-Program Analysis and Evaluation Techniques. Package 6, Module 2. Washington, D.C.: National Training and Development Service Urban Management Curriculum Development Project, 1977. 71 p.

The issue paper technique, from a management by objectives point of view, is taught as a first step in the program analysis process. Key elements to be developed include: the magnitude, pervasiveness, and importance of the problem; public goals and objectives associated with the problem; effectiveness measures for realizing progress toward the problem's resolution; and present potential governmental alternative courses of action. Data on three communities is presented to allow for the development of issue papers.

EXAMPLES OF ISSUE ANALYSIS

Caro, Francis G. AN ANALYSIS OF ADVANTAGES AND DISADVANTAGES OF MAJOR OPTIONS FOR ORGANIZING AND FINANCING A PERSONAL CARE SYSTEM FOR THE ELDERLY DISABLED. Working Paper. Waltham, Mass.: Brandeis University, Florence Heller Graduate School for Advanced Studies in Social Welfare, May 1971. 14 p. Paperbound.

> The author lays out his series of criteria for a system for the personal care of the elderly disabled, including: part of a system also including income maintenance, medical care, and rehabilitation; benefits for the full duration of need adjusted for geographic variation in cost, and related to the extent of functional impairment; the availability of choices among home, community, and institutional care; and politically and eco-nomically feasible costs. Underlying issues for the design of alternatives include: administrative locus; eligibility; form of benefits; and method of financing.

Children's Defense Fund of the Washington Research Project. CHILDREN OUT OF SCHOOL IN AMERICA. Cambridge, Mass.: October 1974. 366 p. Paperbound.

> This is a fine example of issue identification by an advocacy organization, an urban policy version of the work done by the Ralph Nader organizations. Survey research which attempts to quantify the dimensions of the problem is selectively organized and categorized into a policy document which proposes reforms for each of the social problems which are highlighted--barriers to attendance, exclusion of children with special needs, and school discipline.

Christenson, Charles. DISEASE CONTROL PROGRAMS (A): BENEFIT-COST ANALYSIS OF PROGRAM TO ENCOURAGE THE USE OF PROTECTIVE DEVICES BY MOTORCYCLISTS. Boston: Intercollegiate Case Clearing House, n.d. 19 p. 9-112-007.

> The case presents a decision as to whether a cost-benefit analysis

of a particular program should be used to justify the contemplated level of funding of that program. Problems presented in regard to the analysis include: review in exclusively public health terms; some specifically cited cultural biases and assumed cost factors; and exclusion of the possible use of findings based upon new research.

David, Preston. "Report on the Einhorn Matter at Lincoln Hospital." New York: City Commission on Human Rights, July 1971. 25 p. Mimeo.

The removal of a hospital chief of pediatrics led to this investigation into a conflict over the character and practice of community-based medicine at a public hospital. The report addresses questions of ethnic discrimination, community participation, and the application of ideology within a public service system. While not itself an issue analysis, the report lends itself to use as a resource material for teaching the approach.

Drucker, Mark L., ed. "Forest Hills Scattered Site Public Housing Case." Edwardsville: Southern Illinois University at Edwardsville, Graduate Urban Studies Program, September 1975. 239 p. Mimeo.

This is a collection of a great many of the materials needed to conduct an issue analysis of this problem--the press releases and position papers of the different interest groups, some of the reports filed by public agencies on the question, transcripts of television debates held during the crisis, and feature articles from periodicals detailing the facts of the case.

Eisenstadt, Karen. "A Program for Improving City Services to the Aging." Memorandum to the director of the New York City Budget Bureau, 6 October 1972. 24 p. Mimeo.

This is an excellent example of a cost and organizational analysis of institutional versus noninstitutional care alternatives for the elderly. It cuts across agency jurisdictions and concepts special to specific forms of service delivery, to clarify the choices confronting a city.

Fitzgibbons, Stephen B. "Library Department Program Analysis and Review." Report F4-58. Phoenix, Ariz.: Budget and Research Department, May 1974. 58 p. Mimeo.

After reviewing the library system goals, this program analysis proposes policy and program recommendations in a variety of different areas: increasing or varying loan periods; changing branch library service hours; publicizing telephone information services; and marketing usage more energetically.

Fritsky, Stephen J., and Kennedy, Patrick D. ADMINISTRATION OF THE NEW JERSEY STATE CIVIL SERVICE COMMISSION. Report 75-1. Trenton,

N.J.: State Legislature, Office of Fiscal Affairs, Division of Program Analysis, January 1975. 237 p.

> An organizational analysis of the system, in particular in terms of resources and external pressures, is followed by extensive review of classification and compensation, recruitment and examination, and employee performance evaluation and training.

Gill, Richard, with Taylor, Graeme. EMERGENCY AMBULANCE SERVICE (A), (B). Boston: Intercollegiate Case Clearing House, n.d. 40 p. ICH 13C25-6.

> The first of these two cases lays out the organization, manning structure, and volume of calls of this New York City service. It asks for definitions of the system, output measures, and possible alternatives and criteria. The second case requests an assessment of a report called "Simulation and Cost-Effectiveness Analysis of New York's Emergency Ambulance System" by Deputy Administrator Emanuel S. Savas, which illustrates the application of these techniques to a hospital district in Brooklyn.

Harvard University. Graduate School of Business Administration. WALNUT AVENUE CHURCH. Boston: Intercollegiate Case Clearing House, 1972. 5 p. 9-372-293.

> This is a fine sample case to use in applying issue analysis. A church's congregation needed to decide whether its steeple-- damaged by lightning--should be rebuilt or not. Some members felt that the money should be used to fund social causes.

Hendrick, Thomas E., and Plane, Donald R. POLICY ANALYSIS FOR URBAN FIRE STATIONS: HOW MANY AND WHERE (A CASE STUDY OF THE DENVER FIRE DEPARTMENT). Denver: Denver Urban Observatory, November 1974. 17 p. Paperbound.

> The authors describe their analysis of fire services policy, which centered around such alternatives as: maintaining service levels, while either reducing the number of fire companies or keeping the number constant; reducing service levels with an even greater reduction in the number of companies; and increasing both service levels and the number of companies. Response time is viewed as the best measure of the level of service.

Hill, Daniel B., and Breindel, Charles L. ISSUES IN NATIONAL HEALTH INSURANCE. College Park: Pennsylvania State University, Extension Studies 68, April 1977. 38 p. Paperbound.

> This paper is a collection of definitions of the issues on this subject: equity, efficiency, and improved health status goals; and such variables as compulsory versus voluntary approaches, single versus multiple programs, sources of financing, the role of private health insurance companies, comprehensive versus

catastrophic coverage, and features which would alter the health care delivery system.

Irwin, Wallace, Jr., and King, Ellie, eds. ISSUES BEFORE THE 28TH UNITED NATIONS GENERAL ASSEMBLY. New York: United Nations Association of the United States of America, September 1973. 51 p. Paperbound.

> The authors describe their work as a roundup of the resolutions confronting the General Assembly--decisions or recommendations through which the assembly seeks to shape the actions of governments or the opinions of mankind. They view the General Assembly as a factory for global resolutions. Articles discuss such issue areas as human rights, international law, and humanistic development. A discussion of program budgeting at the United Nations is also provided.

Kannensohn, Michael, and Kessler, Nancy J. "Representing the Public Interest: A Report on New Jersey's Department of Public Advocate." STATE GOVERN-MENT 48 (Autumn 1975): 252-56.

> This article details the casework of New Jersey's cabinet level department analyzing and litigating problems on behalf of "the public interest." Particular targets of the agency include: inmate advocacy and parole revocation; rate counsel assistance; mental health advocacy; and dispute settlement of citizen complaints.

Katz, Sam. WELFARE FLAT GRANTS IN PENNSYLVANIA: A CASE STUDY IN ISSUE ANALYSIS. New York: New School for Social Research, Department of Urban Affairs and Policy Analysis, September 1974. 39 p. Paperbound.

> This report combines a strong issue analysis of the welfare flat grants issue then confronting Pennsylvania, with some good description of the organization of the analytic process within a problem-solving laboratory at the New School.

Kooney, Alan. THE NEW JERSEY GREEN ACRES LAND ACQUISITION PRO-GRAM. Report 75-6. Trenton, N.J.: State Legislature, Office of Fiscal Affairs, Division of Program Analysis, November 1975. 90 p.

> The program is analyzed in a context in which the basis for determining needs is extensively reviewed, prior to an assessment of the character of the acquisition processes.

Los Angeles County. FINAL REPORT: COMMUNITY RENEWAL PROGRAM CALIFORNIA R-106 (CR) (6) SECOND AMENDATORY. Los Angeles: Office of the Chief Administrative Officer, June 1970.

> 1. ISSUE PAPER AND PROGRAM ANALYSIS OF ISSUES IN JUVENILE DETENTION. 10 p.

This piece explores the use of program analysis in the case studies and discusses limitations of the approach: weaknesses in both performance measurement and fiscal impact concepts; the need to involve top management; and the tendency to view program analysis as "answers" rather than as illumination of issues.

2. PROGRAM ANALYSIS REPORT: JUVENILE DETENTION FACILITIES CROWDING. 26 p.

Alternatives analyzed are: detention facility expansion; intensive and continuing investigation; and short-term placement in foster care.

3. ISSUES IN JUVENILE DETENTION FACING THE PROBATION DEPARTMENT. 21 p.

This issue paper lays out the juvenile detention problem in terms of capacity and crowding, costs, effects on youth, and impacts upon causes of the problem. Alternatives of the type listed above are detailed, as well as the use of short-term crisis placement and therapeutic detention beds, the decentralization of intake, and the elimination of categories of delinquency.

4. DESCRIPTION OF THE DEVELOPMENT OF THE ISSUE PAPER AND ANALYSIS OF THE LOS ANGELES COUNTY SHERIFF'S PATROL PROGRAM. 6 p.

This paper discusses the process which seemed to show that the point of diminishing returns on free patrol time had been reached, and further resources should be committed to other areas.

5. ANALYSIS REPORT: SHERIFF'S PATROL PROGRAM. 5 p.

This report summarizes the findings mentioned above and provides some basic data illustrating the analysis.

6. ISSUES IN LAW ENFORCEMENT PATROL ACTIVITIES. 15 p.

The issue paper details the basis for analysis of the patrol issue and presents, as alternatives; more effective scheduling; increasing men and cars; and maintaining the present system.

7. DESCRIPTION OF STAFFWORK AND RESULTS ON THE ANALYSIS OF THE PROBLEM OF RECIDIVIST ALCOHOLISM IN THE COUNTY OF LOS ANGELES. 6 p.

Time committed to this analysis broke down as follows: review of literature and departmental reports (35 percent); discussions, meetings, and field visits (25 percent); and draft and report writing, (40 percent). The difficulty of addressing a problem like alcoholism in discussed.

8. THE PROBLEM OF RECIDIVIST ALCOHOLISM IN LOS ANGELES COUNTY. 22 p.

This issue paper lays out alternatives comparing the present system with an ameliorated new version of that system (paraprofessionals and a different kind of "jail") and with decriminalization.

9. ESTIMATED COST TO COUNTY TAXPAYERS DUE TO THE MISUSE OF ALCOHOL, 1968-1969. 11 p.

This is a cost analysis submitted to the board of supervisors which contributed to the program analysis.

McKinsey and Company. CASE EXAMPLE OF A P.P.B. SUBMISSION. New York: City Budget Bureau, 1969. 57 p.

This is an excellent demonstration of the role which issue or program analysis can play in a PPB system. The program narrative for the Department of Sanitation's refuse collection function is presented, followed by a full analysis of the mechanical sweeping issue. Alternatives describe variations in resource allocation and scheduling among districts, at different funding levels.

Manion, Patrick. "Equipment Analysis, Program Analysis and Review." Report 77-24. Phoenix, Ariz.: Budget and Research Department, October 1976. 22 p. Mimeo.

Three alternatives are analyzed. A policy of maintaining the existing replacement level is contrasted against maintaining the desired replacement level and eliminating all overage equipment within three years, and within six years.

Manion, Patrick; Voight, Mark; and Wendt, Jon E. "Police Program Analysis and Review." Report 76-51. Phoenix, Ariz.: Budget and Research Department, February 1976. 157 p. Mimeo.

This program analysis costs out various alternatives demonstrating how the present police response time for nonemergency and emergency calls can be reduced to meet national standards. It also discusses the prevalence of nonemergency and noncriminal calls, and the difficulty of providing "full service" at peak points.

Moore, Mark. "Anatomy of the Heroin Problem: An Exercise in Problem Definition." POLICY ANALYSIS 2 (Fall 1976): 639-62.

This article provides an excellent example of issue definition, as the author demonstrates how to first identify those attributes of the world affected by either heroin use or policies designed to control heroin use. Next he details the public policies directed at affecting the heroin use system, and attempts to lay out the causal variables which will determine the effectiveness of these public policies.

Moscatello, Harry J., and Kennedy, Patrick D. FINANCING AND CON-STRUCTION OF DORMITORIES AND STUDENT CENTERS VIA THE EDUCA-TIONAL FACILITIES AUTHORITY. Report 74-3. Trenton, N.J.: State Legislature, Office of Fiscal Affairs, Division of Program Analysis, June 1974. 82 p.

> The cost and performance aspects of both construction and financing programs are evaluated. The appropriate questions are asked about the utilization and ultimate value to the state of the capital projects.

Moscatello, Harry J., with Smalley, Victoria B. ANALYSIS OF NEW JERSEY'S SEASONAL FARM LABOR PROTECTION PROGRAMS. Report 75-3. Trenton, N.J.: State Legislature, Office of Fiscal Affairs, Division of Program Analysis, May 1975. 47 p.

> This is a useful program analysis case study of the impact of state regulation in a major social policy problem area. It focuses on issues such as inspection, housing, wage protection, and crew leader control.

Muir, William K., Jr. DEFENDING 'THE HILL' AGAINST METAL HOUSES. Inter-University Case Program Case, no. 26. University: University of Alabama, June 1955. 37 p.

> This is the classic New Haven case of the policymaking process surrounding the provision of low-rent, prefabricated houses for 130 families. There is a particularly vivid depiction of the actors in the process. The case provides strong background for the application of issue analysis skills.

Murphy, Serre. "New York City's Partial Tax Exemption Program for New Housing Construction." New York: New School for Social Research, Department of Urban Affairs and Policy Analysis, 1976. 7 p. Mimeo.

> A member of the analytic team which evaluated this program summarizes the relevant data for a decision on continuing or modifying the program. Nine brief and directive tables of data allow for very simple and clear analysis in order to develop conclusions to recommend to the responsible administrator.

Mushkin, Selma J., and Freidin, Ralph. LEAD POISONING IN CHILDREN: THE PROBLEM IN D.C. AND PREVENTIVE STEPS. Washington, D.C.: Georgetown University, Public Services Laboratory, September 1971. 24 p. Paperbound.

> This is a classic example of the development in an issue paper of the policy research required to eventually complete an issue analysis. The summary of the research details: the meaning of

undue absorption and the basis for relevant standards; the size
of the population at risk; and possible health consequences.
Alternative directions to be pursued include: removal of the
hazard; early case finding and prevention; remedial care; and
health education.

New Jersey. Office of Dispute Settlement. "Brief Summary of Office of Dispute Settlement Operations." Trenton, N.J.: State Department of the Public Advocate, 1976. 7 p. Mimeo.

Fact-finding and conflict resolution efforts in this office are
detailed in a discussion of the office's role and in three case
studies of consent agreements: the state resource allocation
formula for federal funds for the aged; a bilingual education
college program dispute; and a housing project-youth violence
controversy.

Newport, Lou. CITY HALL ANALYSIS. Fairview Heights, Ill.: Department
of Planning, 6 September 1977. 10 p.

This memorandum, developed for city council and public review,
examines alternative sites for that community's new city hall,
explicates some engineering costing assumptions, and concludes
with a criteria-choice matrix review of the alternatives.

New York City. Department of City Planning. "The Convention Center: An Analysis." New York: City Planning Commission, October 1973. 19 p. Mimeo.

This is an advocacy analysis supporting the prior decision of city
government to develop a convention center. A series of decision
criteria proposed by opponents are reviewed. They include:
environmental problems; transit problems; destruction of neighborhood character; and funding sources.

Patton, Carl Vernon. "A Seven Day Project: Early Faculty Retirement Alternatives." POLICY ANALYSIS 1 (Fall 1975): 731-53.

This is an example of a short-term issue analysis developed by
a second-year University of California, Berkeley, public policy
student. Alternatives include individual-based early annuity,
group-based early annuity, and partial employment plus early
annuity. The selection of a preferred alternative is based upon
relative weights assigned to criteria, such as least cost, "new
blood," retiree income, and the ability to select retirees.

Reeves, Richard. A FORD, NOT A LINCOLN. New York: Harcourt Brace
Jovanovich, 1975. 212 p.

In chapter 3, the author has published a brief criteria-choice
matrix-style analysis for President Ford on what the future of

community action should be at the Office of Economic Opportunity. The format, rather than the content, is worth noting.

Russell, John, with the help of Briggs, Terrence. DOVER MUNICIPAL HOSPITAL. Boston: Boston University, School of Management, December 1977. 16 p.

This short but complicated case provides the basis for determining clinical and research laboratory policy for a municipal hospital. The city's auditor raises the issue by noting that the hospital is violating a law by doing high volumes of business with outside laboratories without competitive bidding.

Savar, Deborah E., and Westmeyer, Wesley R. SPECIAL PROGRAM ANALYSIS OF UNEMPLOYMENT INSURANCE FRAUD DETECTION AND CONTROL ACTIVITY IN THE NEW JERSEY DIVISION OF UNEMPLOYMENT AND DISABILITY INSURANCE. Report SPA-1. Trenton, N.J.: State Legislature, Office of Fiscal Affairs, Division of Program Analysis, August 1975. 33 p.

This program analysis is a review of the organizational operations and policies of the relevant portions of the unemployment insurance system--the status of the fund and its benefit overpayment recovery activities.

Savas, Emanuel S. "Policy Analysis for Local Government: Public vs. Private Refuse Collection." POLICY ANALYSIS 3 (Winter 1977): 49-74.

This is the classic discussion of alternative municipal refuse collection systems. Alternatives proposed include municipal, contract, franchise, private, and self-service. The author intensively examines the relevant efficiency and economy-of-scale criteria associated with the issue.

Schramm, Richard. ITHACA MUNICIPAL ELECTRIC POWER TASK FORCE REPORT: SUMMARY AND RECOMMENDATIONS. Ithaca, N.Y.: Planning Department of City of Ithaca, 29 June 1977. 24 p.

This analysis costs out the implications of the go-no go decision on potential city acquisition and operation of the local electricity distribution system. Each of the relevant criteria required to make the decision is explored--the city's ability to acquire the system, financing of the acquisition, availability and cost of power, requirements for operation and maintenance, total costs and revenue, financial and economic effects, and non-financial aspects.

Scott, David W. "Issue Paper Series." 5 papers. Springfield, Ill.: Office of Education, State Board of Education, 1977. Mimeo.

Good examples of issue paper development technique are five papers drafted for review for inclusion on the agenda of Illinois's

State Board of Education. Each issue paper thoroughly defines the issue, lays out provisional policy options, and points out what information needs to be obtained and where such information might be found.

The papers are:

"Tenure." 4 p.
"Public Sector Collective Bargaining." 2 p.
"Teacher Education Governance." 3 p.
"Teacher Education Programs." 3 p.
"Early Retirement." 3 p.

System Design Concepts, and Parsons, Brinckerhoff, Quade, and Douglas. WEST SIDE HIGHWAY PROJECT: PRELIMINARY ANALYSIS OF ALTERNATIVE ALIGNMENTS, BROOKLYN BATTERY TUNNEL TO HARRISON STREET. Report 5.02. New York: West Side Highway Project, November 1972. 53 p.

This is the classic analysis of the long-term New York City issue involving construction of either an inboard or an outboard extension of the highway. Key criteria include timing, costs, right-of-way, construction impacts, environmental effects, and legal and financial considerations.

Tomson, Carol Neuman, with Smiley, Victoria, and Woodward, Thurman D., Jr. PROGRAM ANALYSIS OF THE NEW JERSEY PAROLE SYSTEM. Report 75-5. Trenton, N.J.: State Legislature, Office of Fiscal Affairs, Division of Program Analysis, 1975. 125 p.

This program analysis first reviews the organization of the system, and then focuses on sentencing and parole eligibility, the decision-making process, and parole supervision. Recidivism and population flow figures are then reviewed in a context in which costs are also considered.

Ukeles, Jacob B.; Kerner, Steven; and Brawer, Allen. TOWARD A CITYWIDE POLICY GOVERNING THE PRIVATE USE OF PUBLIC STREETS. New York: New School for Social Research, Department of Urban Affairs and Policy Analysis, 28 July 1972. (Draft). 57 p.

This issue analysis looks at New York City policies toward newsstands, sidewalk cafes, and peddlers. Street peddling alternatives include: "getting tough"; banning peddlers from selling manufactured goods while allowing other peddlers to sell food or handicrafts; providing permanent locations; and decentralizing city-wide regulatory authority to a neighborhood level of government.

U.S. American Revolution Bicentennial Administration and U.S. Department of Housing and Urban Development. CHALLENGE/RESPONSE. Washington, D.C.: HUD, 1976. 18 p. Paperbound.

This pamphlet summarizes the content of the series of issue papers on American social policy problems drafted for use as discussion guides for voluntary organizations during the bicentennial. Each paper focuses on a separate "action area" and lays out the issues, the response of some specific American communities, some discussion questions, a bibliography, and a list of organizations involved in addressing the issue.

_____. CITIZEN INVOLVEMENT. Washington, D.C.: HUD, 1976. 17 p.

Responding programs include: COMMUNICATIONS. 25 p.; COMMUNITY DEVELOPMENT. 25 p.; ECONOMIC DEVELOPMENT. 21 p.; ENVIRONMENT. 21 p.; HEALTH. 23 p.; HUMAN VALUES AND UNDERSTANDING. 21 p.; LEARNING. 29 p.; LEISURE. 25 p.; TRANSPORTATION. 21 p.

_____. HORIZONS ON DISPLAY: PART OF THE CONTINUING AMERICAN REVOLUTION. Washington, D.C.: HUD, 1976. Foldout pamphlet.

A map displays listings of the two hundred American programs described in the series. This was the official American demonstration project for habitat, the United Nations Conference on Human Settlements, Vancouver, Canada, from 31 May to 11 June 1976.

Vancil, Richard F. POST OFFICE DEPARTMENT (C). Case 9-111-051. Boston: Intercollegiate Case Clearing House, n.d. 13 p.

This "Postal Holiday Policy" case provides an excellent exercise in issue definition. All of the background data is presented to distinguish the central policy issue from underlying and related issues.

Vaupel, James W. MUDDLING THROUGH ANALYTICALLY. Durham, N.C.: Duke University, Institute of Policy Science and Public Affairs Center for Policy Analysis, May 1973. 28 p.

The author uses examples, such as a decision on a "Zenith City" housing plan, to illustrate his approach to decision theory. He discusses decision trees involving probability assumptions and utility values, and views incomplete analysis as "decomposed intuition." He talks about analysis within a context of intuition and habit, and describes sensitivity analysis, the expected value of perfect information, and raises the premise that analysts should deliberate up to the point where the likely benefits of improving planning are just worth the time and effort of reflection.

_____. USING DECISION ANALYSIS TO STRUCTURE AN ETHICAL DILEMMA. Durham, N.C.: Duke University, Institute of Policy Sciences and Public Affairs, Center for Policy Analysis, May 1975. 26 p.

This is part of the work this author developed in conjunction with

Robert Behn, and is based on Robert Veatch's case in the Hastings Center Report about a woman trying to decide whether to allow herself to conceive when there is a chance that her baby might carry hemophilia. The author approaches this bioethical decision through decision theory.

Vickers, Sir Geoffrey. THE ART OF JUDGMENT. New York: Basic Books, 1965. 242 p.

This distinguished British corporate attorney and public administrator details a series of examples to illustrate some sound conceptualizations about different aspects of the decision situation. For example, he titles chapter 16 "The Elusive Issue" and illustrates how important it is to determine and solve, what is, in fact, the central policy issue. See particularly chapters 14-19.

Weisbrod, Burton A. "Costs and Benefits of Medical Research: A Case Study of Poliomyelitis." JOURNAL OF POLITICAL ECONOMY 79 (May-June 1971): 527-44.

This article provides estimates of research expenditures on polio, forms of productivity benefits from applying the knowledge generated by the researcher, and the costs of applying that knowledge. Internal rates of return are calculated to fall between 4 and 14 percent. The allocative efficiency of private market behavior is discussed, when a collective-consumption good, such as research knowledge, requires the use of an individual-consumption good, such as a vaccination, for its application.

Westmeyer, Wesley R. THE NEW JERSEY URBAN RENEWAL ASSISTANCE PROGRAM. Report 75-2. Trenton, N.J.: State Legislature, Office of Fiscal Affairs, Division of Program Analysis, March 1975. 104 p.

This is an interesting example of how an intergovernmental grants office performs, and what measures might be employed to evaluate its efforts. It is also a view from an unusual source of the impact which a federal program has upon localities.

_____. PROGRAM ANALYSIS OF OFFICE SPACE FOR STATE AGENCIES. Report 73-2. Trenton, N.J.: State Legislature, Office of Fiscal Affairs, Division of Program Analysis, May 1973. 77 p.

This is a systematic study of a classic managerial issue. Property management choices on leased versus owned space are viewed in terms of both quality and utilization considerations. The costs of leased space, of course, receive particular attention, and delays in the leasing process are examined.

Westmeyer, Wesley R., and Savar, Deborah [E.]. PROGRAM ANALYSIS OF BUS AND RAIL SUBSIDIES ADMINISTERED BY THE STATE DEPARTMENT OF

TRANSPORTATION. Report 75-7. Trenton, N.J.: State Legislature, Office of Fiscal Affairs, Division of Program Analysis, December 1975. 164 p.

> A systems analysis of public transportation in the state provides the basis for a review of policy and the roles of different institutions in the policymaking process. The department's functions and administration of subsidies are detailed, and alternative policies are proposed and evaluated for the future.

_____. THE SOUTHWESTERN NEW JERSEY BUSFEEDER SUBSIDY. Report 74-2. Trenton, N.J.: State Legislature, Office of Fiscal Affairs, Division of Program Analysis, February 1974. 97 p.

> The development of the busfeeder subsidy concept is traced, in a context in which dial-a-ride and senior citizen half-fare programs are also discussed. The relationship of automobile driving to bus ridership (for commutation purposes) is assessed.

Wiseman, C. "Selection of Major Planning Issues." POLICY SCIENCES 9 (1978): 71-86.

> The author discusses how to filter issues to determine which require analysis instead of administrative handling. He looks at criteria such as size (resources committed, projected need or demand for service), nature (the range of choice about future courses of action complexity), future implications (type of innovation involving future resource implications, future flexibility, significance of outcome), and political setting (level of urgency, consistency in decision making, strategic relevance or sensitivity, nature and purposes of pressures for change.

COST CRITERIA

Allen, Dwight, and Kingsdale, Jon. A FRAMEWORK FOR CAPITAL CONTROLS
IN HEALTH CARE. Washington, D.C.: Government Research Corp., March
1978. 27 p.

> A model framework for regulating capital investment in health
> care services is proposed as a component of a national cost con-
> tainment strategy. Three phases are recommended: a national
> moratorium on both public and private major capital expenditure;
> a HEW-calculated interim capital expenditure ceiling designed
> to achieve zero net growth in major capital assets; and a five-
> year national capital expenditures ceiling at a congressionally
> determined level, allocated to the states to be implemented
> through their certificate of need programs.

_____. A PROPOSAL FOR STATE RATE-SETTING: LONG-RANGE CONTROLS
ON THE COST OF INSTITUTIONAL HEALTH SERVICES. Washington, D.C.:
Government Research Corp., May 1977. 22 p.

> Federal imposition of a national prospective reimbursement pro-
> gram, to be administered by state commissions on rates and bud-
> gets, is urged. Budgets and rates exceeding state limits would
> be subjected to detailed examination and, if found to be ex-
> cessive, would not be allowed.

Allen, George R., and Roman, Paul N. "Value Engineering and the Department of Defense." In FEDERAL CONTRIBUTIONS TO MANAGEMENT: EFFECTS
ON THE PUBLIC AND PRIVATE SECTORS, edited by David S. Brown, chapter
9. New York: Praeger Publishers, 1971.

> This is a good introductory chapter describing value engineering,
> the technique designed to identify alternative ways of providing
> needed functions at lower costs. Value engineering or value
> analysis, as it is also called, raises such criteria as: Does its
> use contribute value? Are its costs proportionate to its usefulness?
> Does it need all of its features? Will another dependable sup-
> plier provide it for less? Is anyone else buying it for less?

Anthony, Robert N. MANAGEMENT ACCOUNTING PRINCIPLES. Homewood, Ill.: Richard D. Irwin, 1965. 444 p.

> Chapters 15-18 of this classic text are sound basic readings in cost analysis and cost accounting. Chapter 15 distinguishes direct from overhead costs; chapter 16 examines fixed and variable costs; and chapter 17 defines variances. Chapter 18 focuses on those aspects of cost most frequently employed as criteria in decision analysis; e.g., future and differential costs, and full cost and contribution pricing.

Armstrong, Philip A. VOCATIONAL REHABILITATION PROGRAMS UNDERGOING RAPID EXPANSION: A SIMULATION STUDY OF COST AND CASELOAD STATISTICS. Working paper no. 214/RS021. Berkeley: University of California, Institute of Urban and Regional Development, June 1973. 33 p.

> Since the author believes that the observed cost per rehabilitation estimated each fiscal year is a poor indicator of the true costs of rehabilitating the "average" disabled person, he lays out a simulation model more useful for projecting true costs and performance of a program in a period of growth or contraction.

Bagby, Dale Gordon. HOUSING REHABILITATION COSTS. Abstract no. 1. Cambridge: Joint Center for Urban Studies of MIT and Harvard University, 1970. 9 p.

> This thesis is summarized as an abstract report on the costs of "wreck-out" rehabilitating eighty-nine single-family brick row houses in Philadelphia between 1966 and 1968. The costs were found to be 12 to 15 percent cheaper than new construction, and 22 to 24 percent cheaper than new construction in urban renewal projects (including demolition costs).

Balderston, F.E. "Cost Analysis in Higher Education." CALIFORNIA MANAGEMENT REVIEW 17 (Fall 1974): 93-107.

> This article by a former University of California vice-president of planning and analysis, focuses on cost measurement issues: What resources are being employed? How does resource use vary with changes in the volume of activity? Is the pattern of resource use efficient? What is the trend over time? There is also a discussion of "cost reduction versus greater effectiveness in resource use."

Bernstein, Blanche, and Giacchino, Priscilla. "Costs of Day Care: Implications for Public Policy." CITY ALMANAC 6 (August 1971): 1-14.

> This study finds that since 40 to 50 percent of the costs of either acceptable or desirable day care programs are attributable to education, health care, or special services, costs should be charged to these functions, rather than used as an argument

against the potential employment of AFDC mothers. Comparative cost analysis indicates that industry and business firms can deliver slightly less expensive services for their employees. Quality versus quantity trade-offs are explored.

Berry, Ralph E., Jr. "Cost and Efficiency in the Production of Hospital Services." MILBANK MEMORIAL FUND QUARTERLY 52 (Summer 1974): 291-313.

From 1965 to 1967, six thousand hospitals were studied, and a model was developed expressing hospital cost as a function of the level of output, the quality of services provided, the scope of services provided, factor prices, and relative efficiency. The article concludes that quality does affect costs, medical education is a significant factor affecting hospital costs, and "product mix" has a significant impact upon costs. A final discussion characterizes high-cost and low-cost hospitals.

Block, Michael K. COST, SCALE ECONOMIES, AND OTHER ECONOMIC CONCEPTS. Alexandria, Va.: American Bar Association, Correctional Economics Center, February 1976. 52 p.

This monograph empirically estimates the relationship between total average and marginal costs, and particular outputs of California correctional institutions between 1948 and 1964 (community security, medical care training, hotel or housing services). Specifically, changes in the production of hotel services at San Quentin and Folsom prisons are reviewed in terms of their effects upon total costs. By what percentage does a population increase change costs? Are cost increases larger or smaller with a 2,500 population than with a 4,500 population? Will a more violence-prone group require proportionately greater expenditures? Will building excess capacity into a prison lead to higher--not lower--costs in the future?

Brook, Robert H., and Davies-Avery, Allyson. QUALITY ASSURANCE AND COST CONTROL IN AMBULATORY CARE. Paper P-5817. Santa Monica, Calif.: Rand Corp., July 1977. 32 p.

This essay discusses many of the aspects of quality assurance in the delivery of ambulatory care which are potentially cost-intensive: referral to modal specialists; reliance upon technical processes to the detriment of the "art of care"; board certification; and the typical organization of medical practice.

Bruce-Briggs, Barry. "'Child Care': The Fiscal Time Bomb." PUBLIC INTEREST 49 (Fall 1977): 87-102.

This muckraking attack on American day care policies focuses on the determinants of cost: standards in facilities and staff-child ratios; staff qualifications; and other concepts obviously

galling to the author. On the other hand, there is good discussion of the values underlying costs, such as the choice between family home care, nursery school, and day care, and
assumptions about the ability of the poor to educate their own
children.

Burchell, Robert W., and Listokin, David. THE FISCAL IMPACT HANDBOOK:
PROJECTING THE LOCAL COSTS AND REVENUES RELATED TO GROWTH.
New Brunswick, N.J.: Rutgers University, Center for Urban Policy Research,
1978. 542 p.

The authors, after extensive analyses of the impact of individual
projects and HUD sponsorship of further research, have produced
the basic text needed to cost out such basic planning decisions
as new land development and annexation. Cost-estimation
methods which are detailed include average cost approaches
such as "per capita multiplier," "service standard," and proportional valuation," and case study, "comparable city," and
"employment anticipation" marginal cost approaches.

Cole, George F., and Greenberger, Howard L. "Staff Attorneys vs. Judicare:
A Cost Analysis." JOURNAL OF URBAN LAW 50 (1973): 705-16.

In Meriden, Connecticut, nine hundred welfare clients were
given the choice, during a three-year period, of taking legal
problems to a two-person neighborhood legal service office, or
to any one of the forty members of the private bar in that city
(Judicare). Given the disposition of Judicare attorneys to
charge their minimum fee (rather than costing out the actual
time they spent on cases), the legal services approach costs out
quite favorably in comparison.

Correia, Eddie. "Public Certification of Need for Health Facilities." AMERICAN
JOURNAL OF PUBLIC HEALTH 65 (March 1975). 260-65.

The article discusses how the certification of need approach is
designed to reduce costs by preventing the construction of facilities that will be underutilized, and by "influencing treatment
patterns to be more efficient." It further details the theoretical
basis for regulation, the estimation techniques employed in trying
to determine the "right" number of beds, and the implementation
problems likely to result from attempts to operationalize the
approach.

Cotton, David L. URBAN SCHOOL DESEGREGATION COSTS. St. Louis:
Washington University, Center for Educational Field Studies, November 1977.
60 p.

Five cities involved in the desegregation process were studied--
Buffalo, Cleveland, Columbus, Dayton, and Milwaukee. "Net
local cost" is defined as the difference between gross expenditures

for desegregation and (a) new state and federal financial assistance, and (b) cost savings such as those accruing from any school closings. The principal components of total cost include: transportation, educational program improvements, including staff training; facilities remodeling and renovation; public information and community relations programs; and litigation.

Culliton, Barbara J. "Health Care Economics: The High Cost of Getting Well." SCIENCE 200 (26 May 1978): 883-85.

The writer argues in this popular piece that all aspects of the uncoordinated and decentralized system buy "the best" without regard to cost, and that there have been no effective incentives to hold costs down. Hemodialysis is cited as an example. Costs are attributed to such factors as hospital and physicians' wages, the oversupply of hospital beds, overspecialization in medical practice, expensive new "high" technology, and third-party payment processes.

Das, Amiya K. REDUCING HOUSING COSTS. Technical paper no. 3. Tallahassee: Florida, State Department of Community Affairs, Division of Technical Assistance, July 1977. 40 p.

Since the increase in median price of a single-family home in Florida has been disproportionately greater than the rise in income level of the average household in that state, this agency proposes measures which it believes will help to reduce costs. There are recommendations involving zoning law reforms, elimination of unnecessary governmental regulations and standards, reforms in codes, more careful subdivision planning, and better quality control in construction.

Eaves, Elsie. HOW THE MANY COSTS OF HOUSING FIT TOGETHER. Research report no. 16. Washington, D.C.: National Commission on Urban Problems, 1969. 103 p.

This Douglas Commission report records basic average or median housing cost experience for both single-family detached houses and multiunit apartments. In 1966 terms, it identifies how much it costs to buy, finance, build, and operate housing. The report particularly focuses on land, labor, and capitalization costs, in the context of the then-active federal subsidy programs.

Eisenstadt, Karen. FACTORS AFFECTING MAINTENANCE AND OPERATING COSTS IN PRIVATE RENTAL HOUSING. Report R-1055-NYC. New York: New York City Rand Institute, August 1972. 122 p.

This study examines the relationships between structural design, building age, and the annual costs of supplying rental housing. It analyzes the pattern of maintenance and operating expenditures reported by owners of a selected group of pre-1947 multiple

dwellings in New York City, and establishes a typology of
building configurations. The single most important variable in
determining operating and maintenance costs per unit was found
to be the average number of rooms per apartment, which affects
payroll, heating, and repairs and maintenance costs.

Feldstein, Martin. "The High Cost of Hospitals--And What To Do About It."
PUBLIC INTEREST 48 (Summer 1977): 40-54.

The author views the cost question as the central national health
care policy issue. He contends that conventional explanations
as to the cause of the problem are incorrect. Labor costs have
decreased as a fraction of the total hospital bill. "Inefficiency"
is unlikely to account for much of the increase. Technical
progress has been demonstrated, although unlike conditions in
other industries, it has not reduced costs. Instead, he writes
that the high cost of care induces families to buy more complete
insurance, and the growth of insurance induces the hospital to
produce more expensive care.

Fisher, Gene H. "Cost Considerations in Policy Analysis." POLICY ANALYSIS
3 (Winter 1977): 107-14.

Cost analysts are urged to broaden their interpretation of economic costs to better reflect multi-year budget allocation considerations. Negative economic costs should be addressed in
terms of pricing policies, which include pickup of the costs of
environmental health, safety, and other externalities. Distributional effects should be more clearly portrayed.

Frieden, Bernard J. "The New Housing-Cost Problem." PUBLIC INTEREST
49 (Fall 1977): 70-86.

Families with near-average incomes have lost purchasing power
for single-family homes since 1970. Land purchase and development costs, mortgage interest rates, fuel and utilities,
property taxes, and maintenance and repair costs have been
particularly significant in affecting these conditions. The federal
government has destabilized housing and credit markets in its
efforts to relieve inflationary pressures on other sectors of the
economy. In the author's view, the federal government should
review the effects of its own policies upon the cost of housing,
and change its policies accordingly. It should also take positive
action to stabilize production levels by, for example, using
low-income housing production programs to offset cyclical instability, and by offering cash subsidies or tax credits to homebuyers to reduce their down payments during slump periods.

Goldstein, Joyce. WHAT PRICE HEALTH? THE CRISIS BEHIND MEDICAL
INFLATION. Washington, D.C.: Health Service Action, October 1977. 22 p.

The author notes that cost increases have not been matched by commensurate change in the health status of the American people. She traces the problem to cost-plus basis reimbursement patterns by the insurance companies, the relative absence of coverage for outpatient and preventive services, surplus beds, and physicians. She discusses such conventional solutions as cutbacks, planning, and health maintenance organizations, and reviews the national health insurance proposals.

Griffith, John R.; Hancock, Walton M.; and Munson, Fred C. "Practical Ways to Contain Hospital Costs." HARVARD BUSINESS REVIEW 51 (November-December 1973): 131-39.

The writers discuss four areas of cost containment: planning of facilities and services; scheduling of patients and patient services; medical control of facilities utilization and quality of service; and administrative control of manpower and expenditures. They urge community-wide planning, including the elimination of competition between institutions, firm control of the community bed supply, and negotiated incentive or prospective reimbursement schemes for hospitals.

Haggart, Sue A. PROGRAM COST ANALYSIS IN EDUCATIONAL PLANNING. Paper P-4744. Santa Monica, Calif.: Rand Corp., December 1971. 40 p.

This paper develops a planning-cost model for estimating program cost for use in evaluating alternative programs. Haggart feels that "cost per student" and "cost per unit of achievement" ratios are too often used as the outputs of cost-effectiveness analysis, and instead lays out an approach which determines "comparable replication cost," a comparable cost which normalizes the cost of programs. The model detailed is a simple pencil-and-paper operation which effectively categorizes each of the elements as "acquisition" and "operational" costs. With a full set of charts and diagrams, this short piece has excellent applicability to a wide variety of public service areas.

Harvard University. Business School. THE DUKE POWER COMPANY: A FEASIBILITY STUDY IN LOW AND MODERATE INCOME HOUSING. Case 4-670-022, IM 1949R. Boston: Intercollegiate Case Clearing House, 1970. 35 p.

While this case provides a generally useful feasibility study for review, a special highlight is exhibit A of appendix A, a clear cost analysis of a sample multifamily residential project, sorting out unit sizes and space, detailing carrying and amortization costs, and demonstrating projected rent, cash flow, and return on investment.

_____. NOTE ON COSTING ALTERNATIVE CHOICES. Case 9-155-002, EA-C 353R3. Boston: Intercollegiate Case Clearing House, 1965. 22 p.

> This is an excellent reference source, specifically designed to demonstrate how to employ cost criteria in a decision analysis. Future, differential, and opportunity costs are explained. Simple examples, such as the operation of an automobile, are provided, and five brief supplemental problems are posed.

Havighurst, Clark C. "Controlling Health Care Costs." JOURNAL OF HEALTH POLITICS, POLICY AND LAW 1 (Winter 1977): 471-98.

> This article which was adapted from testimony before the Council on Wage and Price Stability, proposes private sector controls appropriate for the health insurance industry. The author discusses coverage limitations and plan-initiated reviews to exclude nonessential care, as well as wider use of fixed indemnity payments or negotiated fees and charges (instead of the payment of usual or customary rates or incurred costs). He suggests that antitrust laws may need to be enforced to combat doctors' resistance to measures of this sort.

Hill, Daniel B. "Identification of Hospital Cost Determinants: A Health Planning Perspective." INQUIRY 13 (March 1976): 61-70.

> The article, in a literature review, identifies what the writer views as planning-relevant variables for cost containment within regional comprehensive health plans. It examines health insurance, other health resources, medical care organization, patient mix, hospital size, and service availability considerations.

Hudes, Karen, and Monkman, Gail S. COMMUNITY PROGRAMS FOR WOMEN OFFENDERS: COST AND ECONOMIC CONSIDERATIONS. Alexandria, Va.: American Bar Association, Correctional Economics Center, June 1975. 53 p.

> This piece is designed to illustrate comparative cost issues in the debate over institutional incarceration versus community-based corrections for women offenders. Using Washington, D.C., as a case study, cost is studied in terms of incarceration, halfway houses, dependent child care, vocational training, and education.

Jones, F. Ron. COST ANALYSIS OF ALTERNATIVE TRANSPORTATION SYSTEMS FOR THE HANDICAPPED. Working paper no. 256. Berkeley: University of California, Institute of Urban and Regional Development, July 1975. 74 p.

> Alternative ways of improving the mobility of 7 million physically disabled Americans are discussed: curb modification; wheelchairs; modified automobiles and vans; fixed-route transit systems; demand-responsive systems; and mobility counseling. Cost analysis conducted by the author indicates that retrofitting

subways and buses and building accessibility into new subway systems are not cost-effective approaches. He proposes that elements of the other programs he discusses be combined into a five-year $5.6 billion package.

Kite, Robert, and Steckler, Ann. "A Cost Analysis Strategy for Education." EDUCATIONAL TECHNOLOGY 14 (July 1974): 49-56.

The article presents a linear planning model to be used in analyzing the economics of education. The model adapts the basic efficiency model used in economic price theory, and graphically portrays the relationship among variables and constraints. A series of examples is provided.

Koehler, John E., and Slighton, Robert L. ACTIVITY ANALYSIS AND COST ANALYSIS IN MEDICAL SCHOOLS. Paper P-4954. Santa Monica, Calif.: Rand Corp., February 1973. 36 p.

This paper details an approach designed to provide activity analysis (what inputs are required to achieve given output targets) and cost analysis (how costs should be assigned to particular processes). The authors argue that even if, in a medical center, activities are too interdependent to allow for determination of the "true" cost of particular outputs, cost data can still be properly organized for decision-making purposes. The paper summarizes an extensive literature of health center cost analysis studies, all influenced by the joint cost dilemma: classic costfinding studies, such as have been developed by the Association of American Medical Colleges; cost estimation with regression analysis; simulation of school activities; and input-output analysis.

Kotelchuck, Ronda. "Government Cost Control Strategies." HEALTH/PAC BULLETIN 75 (March-April 1977): 1-6.

The author suggests that current regulatory processes are important in ultimately controlling costs, because of the public popularity of the character and organization of the new technology-dominant system. Cutbacks, as in New York, are likely to be targeted at what is viewed as more politically and medically marginal ambulatory and preventive care programs. New ideology from very different sources argues for decreased expectations from medical care. The author suggests a focus not upon the level of cost, but upon the allocation of funds--how they are spent and what they buy.

Lave, Judith R., and Leinhardt, Samuel. "The Cost and Length of a Hospital Stay." INQUIRY 13 (December 1976): 327-43.

The writers analyzed a year's data from a Pittsburgh teaching hospital, all individual patient billing records, and discharge file data including demographics, surgical procedures undertaken, admitting status, and discharge diagnosis. Comfortingly enough, the variables that reflected the patients' medical conditions were found to be the most important factors influencing length of stay.

Long, Hugh W. UPTON UNIVERSITY HOSPITAL: CASE STUDY IN HOSPITAL FINANCIAL MANAGEMENT. Chicago: Hospital Research and Educational Trust, 1973. Student Manual: 36 p. Instructor's Guide: 20 p.

This case features the data required to consider a capital budgeting issue confronting a teaching hospital. Students must compare net present value versus internal rate of return outcomes, and see the need to exclude interest costs, depreciation, and reallocated overhead from funds flow determinations. These projections must take into account factors such as inflation, variability in interest rates, third-party reimbursement payment, and delay in the construction process.

Lozano, Eduardo E. "Technical Report: Housing Costs and Alternative Cost Reducing Policies." JOURNAL OF THE AMERICAN INSTITUTE OF PLANNERS 37 (May 1972): 176-81.

This article analyzes the structure of housing costs (including shelter, operating, and total housing costs), and tests the cost-reduction consequences of policies affecting such factors as interest rates, property taxes, and land, improvement, and construction costs. The only single factor which could drastically reduce costs is a policy of practically interest-free mortgage loans, but the industrialization of the construction process would have a 1:4 multiplier effect.

McCaffree, Kenneth. "The Cost of Mental Health Care." INTERNATIONAL JOURNAL OF PSYCHIATRY 4 (August 1967): 142-64.

The differential costs between custodial and intensive treatment institutions are viewed in terms of average cost per patient measures (length of stay times costs per capita per unit of time). The author argues for intensive therapy and rehabilitative care approaches.

Marmor, Theodore R.; Wittman, Donald A.; and Heagy, Thomas C. "The Politics of Medical Inflation." JOURNAL OF HEALTH POLITICS, POLICY AND LAW 1 (Spring 1976): 69-84.

This article examines four medical inflation concepts: absolute and relative price inflation; total real expenditures growth per capita; and relative expenditure growth. It then reviews three types of cures: improving the market; public utility regulation; and effective nationalization of the industry. The authors argue a "political market" theory of imbalanced political interests, concentrated versus diffuse benefits and costs, and suggest that, in fact, the government may not be able to restrain health care expenditures significantly.

Massell, Adele P., and Williams, Albert P. COMPARING COSTS OF IN-PATIENT CARE IN TEACHING AND NON-TEACHING HOSPITALS: METHOD-OLOGY AND DATA. Report R-2027-HEW. Santa Monica, Calif.: Rand Corp., June 1977. 86 p.

> Program cost and production cost analyses are contrasted to il-luminate discussion of higher costs in teaching hospitals, the validity of claims from such institutions, and the appropriate basis for cost burden-sharing among education, patient care, and research programs in teaching hospitals.

Massey, Hugh G.; Novick, David; and Peterson, Richard E. COST MEASURE-MENT: TOOLS AND METHODOLOGY FOR COST EFFECTIVENESS ANALYSIS. Report P-4762. Santa Monica, Calif.: Rand Corp., February 1972. 27 p.

> This essay is an excellent basic source on the subject of cost criteria. First, the authors distinguish the differences between research and development, initial investment, and systems opera-tions costs. Then, there follows discussions of multiyear cost analysis, total program and incremental costing, and the appli-cation of cost-estimating relationships. Sensitivity analysis is also clearly explained.

Merewitz, Leonard. "On Measuring the Efficiency of Public Enterprises: Bus Operating Companies in the San Francisco Bay Area." TRANSPORTATION 6 (March 1977): 45-55.

> Statistical cost functions, nationally estimated, are employed as a basis of comparison for local bus systems services. They are used, according to the author, to establish a range within which the costs of an efficient bus service should fall.

Nader, Ralph, and Green, Mark. "Don't Pay Those High Legal Bills." NEW YORK TIMES MAGAZINE, 20 November 1977, pp. 52-87.

> This popular magazine piece attacks the rate structure and costing analysis characteristic of the major law firms. For example, the setting of "guideline rates" by the law firms is described as a highly subjective set of determinations. The authors claim that lawyers are insensitive to excessive costs reflected in such prac-tices as first-class travel.

Needles, Belverd, Jr. BONNINGTON COMMUNITY HOSPITAL: CASE STUDY IN HOSPITAL FINANCIAL MANAGEMENT. Chicago: Hospital Research and Educational Trust, 1971. Student Manual: 22 p. Instructors's Guide: 22 p.

> This case requires the financial analysis of hospital statements, and a forecasting of the future of the hospital's financial position,

based upon that data. Analysis is needed in order to determine how both to maintain present operations and to finance an expansion program. The case focuses on cash flow, net income, and depreciation, and requires an examination of such indicators as current ratio, quick ratio, current assets to fixed assets, sales to accounts receivable, and total liabilities to total assets.

Newhouse, Joseph P. THE ECONOMICS OF GROUP PRACTICE. Report P-4478/1. Santa Monica, Calif.: Rand Corp., January 1972. 26 p.

This paper discusses how the costs of outpatient medical practice vary with the size of the group providing services. For example, the nonphysician costs of two very large and one quite small clinic are compared with the overhead costs of the private physician. The writer argues theoretically and demonstrates empirically that cost-sharing in group practice raises costs. These findings contradict the conventional wisdom that group practice enhances economies of scale, productivity, and quality of care.

New York State Moreland Act Commission on Nursing Homes and Residential Facilities. REIMBURSING OPERATING COSTS: DOLLARS WITHOUT SENSE. Albany, N.Y.: 1976. 143 p.

This report addresses the state's Medicaid reimbursement problems by proposing a new approach to rate-setting called "efficient care standards." It commends the state for attempting to reimburse full costs, rather than imposing an artificial flat rate. All of the basic information needed for proper cost analysis is not however required from the nursing homes. The costs of many elements of care are not known in any useable form. Increases in rates should be reasonably related to the costs of efficient production of services.

Northrup, David E. "Management's Cost in Public Sector Collective Bargaining." PUBLIC PERSONNEL MANAGEMENT 5 (September-October 1976): 328-34.

This article proposes that management should analyze all of the costs of contract administration, as it participates in collective bargaining negotiations. Apart from direct costs, other concepts which are introduced are "measurable costs," associated with factors such as reduction in force, contracting out, and grievances, and "indirect costs," increased costs associated with the loss of management prerogatives.

Peat, Marwick, Mitchell and Co. COST/SAVING ANALYSIS OF ADMINISTRATIVE IMPROVEMENTS IN THE NEW YORK CITY CRIMINAL COURT. New York: Economic Development Council, March 1973. 62 p.

The consultants review cost information to measure the financial implications of administrative improvements in the courts. They find net annual savings of over $6 million, as well as one-time savings of over $48 million, attributable to reduction of the court backlog. The report represents a good summary of how accountants may estimate and report public agency cost data.

Public Citizen's Health Research Group. THE $8 BILLION HOSPITAL BED OVERRUN: A CONSUMER'S GUIDE TO STOPPING WASTEFUL CONSTRUC-TION. Washington, D.C.: Health Research Group, 1975. 98 p.

This muckraking piece, drafted by Barry Ensminger, proposes that projections of future demand be examined to determine whether geographic boundaries are being manipulated, whether figures demonstrating occupancy rates have been inflated, whether current rates of usage are appropriate bases for future projections, whether all possible, approved local beds have been counted, and whether population growth projections are realistic.

Rausch, Erwin. "Overhead Allocation: Science or Politics?" MANAGEMENT REVIEW 62 (May 1973): 4-8.

This is a good, brief background piece on the subject of determining proportionate contribution to fixed costs within an organization. The writer indicates that new products (or services) are particularly vulnerable to the assumptions employed in allocating overhead costs.

Richmond, Mark S. "Measuring the Cost of Correctional Services." CRIME AND DELINQUENCY 18 (July 1972): 243-52.

This article begins by laying out the estimated national average costs of "criminal careers" reported to the President's Crime Commission in 1965. The author argues that cost analyses are useful in prompting longer looks at such possible reforms as emphasizing more selectivity in the assignment of punishment; relating corrections processes more carefully to outcomes; and "the redesign of vehicles delivering services."

Rydell, C. Peter. FACTORS AFFECTING MAINTENANCE AND OPERATING COSTS IN FEDERAL PUBLIC HOUSING PROJECTS. Paper R-634-NYC. Santa Monica, Calif.: Rand Corp., December 1970. 74 p.

From 1951 to 1967, operating and maintenance costs rose 5.3 percent per year, against a 1.67 percent annual consumer price index increase, and an average 3 percent increase in rent per year. These expenses represent slightly more than half of the cost of New York City's public housing. The author finds that there are significant economies of scale associated with large projects, but no net economies of scale associated with building size. While larger apartments are more expensive to run, the cost increase is less than proportional to the increase in size. Multiple regression analysis also indicates that price inflation, deterioration, and changes in quantity and/or efficiency of service are also significant cost factors.

Singer, Neil M., and Wright, Virginia B. COST ANALYSIS OF CORREC-
TIONAL STANDARDS: INSTITUTIONAL-BASED PROGRAMS AND PAROLE.
2 vols. Alexandria, Va.: American Bar Association, Correctional Economics
Center, January 1976. 21 p.; 162 p.

> These volumes cost out the standards defined by the 1973 Na-
> tional Advisory Commission on Criminal Justice Standards and
> Goals. The summary volume lays out the general implications
> of the findings and identifies the bottom line; while the second
> volume, detailing the cost analysis, provides some good general
> examples of how to cost out new human service programs. Pro-
> grams analyzed include custody, parole, education and training,
> work experience, work release and furloughs, and grievance
> and legal access rights.

Smith, Judy; Homeier, Lynn; and Fineberg, Harvey. BETH ISRAEL HOSPITAL
AMBULATORY CARE (A), (B). Cases C16-75-004-5. Cambridge, Mass.:
Harvard University, Kennedy School of Government, 1976. 40 p.

> The first case lays out the policymaking environment (internal
> and external to the hospital) surrounding Beth Israel's decision
> to restructure its ambulatory services. The second case illus-
> trates the role which "cost-revenue center" planning can play
> in allowing a hospital to commit itself to accelerating its am-
> bulatory services delivery.

Smith, Ralph E. FOREGONE EARNINGS DURING MANPOWER TRAINING.
Paper 350-11. Washington, D.C.: Urban Institute, January 1970. 21 p.

> The paper lays out a model to be used in estimating the earn-
> ings which manpower program trainees may forego while they
> complete their training. The model, a good demonstration of
> how to apply one prototypical form of cost criteria, is applied
> to institutional training made available under the Manpower De-
> velopment and Training Act. In terms of manpower benefit-cost
> analysis, the paper attacks the conventional wisdom that fore-
> gone earnings are quite small, and instead argues that these
> costs are the largest costs associated with delivering the programs.

Sparer, Gerald; Okada, Louise M.; and Tillinghast, Stanley. "How Much Do
Family Planning Programs Cost?" FAMILY PLANNING PERSPECTIVES 5
(Spring 1973): 100-106.

> The article is an exercise in empirically determining average
> direct costs of service delivery. Two studies--by Westinghouse
> and by National Analysts, respectively--are reviewed and found
> to come in with very similar average costs per patient. Espe-
> cially good predictors of unit costs are measures of project size
> (patient load and total operating expenditures) and the number
> of years a program has been operating.

Sweeny, Allen, and Wisner, John N., Jr. "Budgeting Basics: A How-To Guide for Managers; Budget Control Through Responsibility Centers." SUPER-VISORY MANAGEMENT 20 (February 1975): 11-22.

>The authors trace the evolution of revenue, cost, and profit center concepts, citing the pressures associated with these approaches for short-range rather than long-range profitability. Measures must be designed to provide for centralized control over disinvestments, and for transfer prices. Return-on-investment centers are also described in the context of long-range versus short-range interest trade-offs, and the residual income approach (charging centers for their use of capital) is described.

_____. "Budgeting Basics: A How-To Guide for Managers; Types of Costs and Their Behavior." SUPERVISORY MANAGEMENT 20 (April 1975): 20-32.

>This is a simple introductory piece describing costs--fixed, variable, and semivariable; direct and indirect--and material, labor, and overhead. Clear charts illustrate, for example, the basics for cost classification: how maintenance, a semivariable cost, varies with the number of units manufactured; and how variable costs such as raw materials vary with the number of units manufactured, and sales commissions with the number of units sold.

Thalheimer, Donald J. COST ANALYSIS OF CORRECTIONAL STANDARDS: HALFWAY HOUSES. 2 vols. Alexandria, Va.: American Bar Association, Correctional Economics Center, October 1975. 19 p.; 134 p.

>Four types of costs are described: criminal justice system costs; costs external to the criminal justice system, borne by individual groups providing services to these clients; opportunity costs incurred by residents; and costs to the community in which the house is located. In the second volume, there is extensive discussion of variations in costs and the causes of such variations; differences in the services provided; availability of resources; interregional cost differentials; and economics of scale and factor indivisibilities.

Trisko, Eugene M., and Shomo, Elwood W. "A Study in Fire Department Cost Allocation." GOVERNMENTAL FINANCE 3 (November 1974): 24-36.

>Two Robert R. Nathan Associates demonstrate the application of cost allocation techniques to motor vehicle fires, as an example of the delivery of fire department services. Both incremental and fully distributed approaches to cost allocation are discussed. In employing the latter, each type of response is assigned a portion of total costs. Motor vehicle fires are viewed in terms of their proportion of total emergency responses, as well as in terms of the proportion of man-hours they demand.

Ulrey, Ivon W. "The Accountant's Role in Cost/Output Analysis." FEDERAL ACCOUNTANT 22 (June 1973): 40-46.

> The author illustrates how managers of food centers can use cost analysis not only to establish standards among their operations at different sites, but also to predict additional costs likely to be associated with increased demand.

U.S. Comptroller General. STUDY OF HEALTH FACILITIES CONSTRUCTION COSTS. Report to the 92d Cong., 2d sess. Washington, D.C.: Senate Committee on Labor and Public Welfare and the House Committee on Interstate and Foreign Commerce, December 1972. 888 p.

> This report examines design, material, and construction process costs, then offers life-cycle cost analysis of selected innovations, and concludes with a discussion of the impact of significant reduction in demand.

U.S. Department of Health, Education and Welfare. CONTROLLING THE COST OF HEALTH CARE. DHEW publication no. (HRA) 77-3182. Hyattsville, Md.: National Center for Health Services Research, Health Resources Administration, Public Health Services, May 1977. 22 p.

> Cost containment is viewed as the central constraint on the achievement of the basic positive goals of the health system. Cost containment strategies are not neutral as to which objectives should receive more or less priority (e.g., quality of care versus equity of access). This report reviews the literature on certificates of need, federal hospital investment assistance, changes in treatment patterns, the effects of insurance, physician and hospital reimbursement, and the character of demand.

U.S. Department of Housing and Urban Development. TASK FORCE ON HOUSING COSTS: INTERIM REPORT. Washington, D.C.: 8 July 1977. 21 p.

> A task force staff and a central office working group met for seven days in June of 1977 to evaluate eighty cost-reducing ideas according to the following criteria: cost impact; feasibility; whether HUD could act to implement it without congressional legislation; and whether the idea should be studied further. The cost reduction ideas were grouped into the following categories: local land use controls, state and local building codes, HUD-FHA processing, HUD environmental reviews, financing costs generally (and the secondary markets in particular), settlement costs, and large-scale land acquisition and development.

Watkins, Ann M. COST ANALYSIS OF CORRECTIONAL STANDARDS: PRE-TRIAL DIVERSION. 2 vols. Alexandria, Va.: American Bar Association, Correctional Economics Center, October 1975. 22 p.; 87 p.

> The first volume lays out and discusses some basic concepts such

as average cost at design capacity per client year and per client, average cost at actual capacity per client year and per client, and average cost per "successfully" terminated client. The second volume proposes a typology of costs: criminal justice system, external, direct and indirect, and opportunity. It then details the breakout of these costs for both drug and employment diversion programs.

Weil, Peter A. "Comparative Costs to the Medicare Program of Seven Prepaid Group Practices and Controls." MILBANK MEMORIAL FUND QUARTERLY/ HEALTH AND SOCIETY 54 (Summer 1976): 339-65.

Open market and prepaid group practice costs to the Medicare program are compared. Administrators of prepaid group practices explain their policies in regard to organizational sponsorship, incentive structure, pattern of selectivity of patients, and re-source availability. Enrollees in prepaid groups incur higher physician costs, but overall these programs demonstrate savings in provider-initiated services (except for home health care). Relatively small, yet hospital-based groups demonstrate the greatest cost savings to Medicare.

Weisberg, Susan. COST ANALYSIS OF CORRECTIONAL STANDARDS: AL-TERNATIVES TO ARREST. 2 vols. Alexandria, Va.: American Bar Associa-tion, Correctional Economics Center, October 1975. 17 p.; 96 p.

This study demonstrates that citation activities will have cost advantages over traditional arrests, if a broad base of eligibility is established for release; if a substantial percentage of those eligible are, in fact, released; and if effective screening and notification procedures keep rates of failure to a minimum. Case flow cost analysis measures are developed in terms of trans-portation to station house; booking; custody to arraignment; and location and prosecution of those who fail to appear.

Whiteneck, Gale G. THE STATE OF THE ART IN DEFINING SOCIAL SER-VICES, DEVELOPING SERVICE UNITS, AND DETERMINING UNIT COSTS, WITH AN ANNOTATED BIBLIOGRAPHY. Denver: University of Denver, Re-search Institute, January 1976. 25 p.

Four basic ratios are proposed for determining unit costs: cost per case, cost per client receiving a specific service, cost per service output, and cost per service time.

COST AND PERFORMANCE CRITERIA

Abt, Clark C. "Forecasting the Cost-Effectiveness of Educational Incentives." EDUCATIONAL TECHNOLOGY 14 (March 1974): 27-29.

> Incentives are being considered for the purposes of increasing such factors as: classroom, school, and school system innovation; the rate of technology transfer; management performance; teacher instructional performance; and student learning performance. The author lays out a list of potential recipients, the forms of incentives which might motivate them, and measures which could demonstrate effective performance (both output and impact measures). He also provides examples of how to "forecast by analogy" the effectiveness of specific incentive programs.

Allison, Graham T. THE MASSACHUSETTS MEDICAL SCHOOL. Kennedy School of Government. Boston: Intercollegiate Case Clearing House, 1975. Case 9-378-556: 110 p.; case sequel 9-378-557: 5 p.; teaching note 5-378-558: 22 p.

> These teaching materials were developed to illustrate the relationship of political feasibility and implementation criteria to more traditional cost and performance criteria. The basic case includes an eighty-eight-page report evaluating the costs and benefits of five alternative proposals for the development of a University of Massachusetts medical school. A second analysis, a sixteen-page in-house analysis, provides additional recommendations, as to how performance criteria should be weighed, and also as to the validity of the arguments of the more extensive work. The case sequel provides a press release announcing the governor's decision. The teaching note lays out the Kennedy School's standards for the development of sound program analysis through a series of questions to be posed against both the professionals' analysis, and the student work to be undertaken in conjunction with the series of cases.

Anderson, Martin. THE FEDERAL BULLDOZER. New York: McGraw-Hill Paperbacks, 1967. 272 p.

Originally published in 1964, this work was regarded as a devastating attack on the logic and the performance of the urban renewal program. Quoting Aristotle, the author argued: "Even when laws have been written down, they ought not always to remain unaltered." However, deserting Aristotle, he urges the program's repeal. The analysis closely examines land-use consequences, sources of funding, tax implications, effects on the national economy, and the extent of the impact upon the quality of available housing.

Anderson, Robert W. "Towards a Cost-Benefit Analysis of Police Activity." PUBLIC FINANCE 29 (1974): 1-18.

The author discusses both apprehension-detections and preventions as benefits, and examines the consequences of the solution of a crime in terms of: a reduction in direct suffering seriousness as evaluated by a group; a change in the number and seriousness of crimes committed by the criminal responsible for crime; and a deterrent effect through fewer crimes committed by others. There is also a discussion of the implications of cost-benefit thinking for service delivery resource allocation policies (relating to the work of Shoup and Mehay, Dosser, and Thurow).

Averous, Christian; Stahl, Konrad; and Cole, Charles. COST BENEFIT ANALYSIS OF REHABILITATION SERVICES PROGRAMS: A FIRST MODEL AND ITS SENSITIVITY ANALYSIS. Working paper 163/RS001. Berkeley: University of California, Institute of Urban and Regional Development, November 1971. 34 p.

The researchers employ sensitivity analysis to evaluate the quality of their application of Conley's cost-benefit approach (see p. 51) to vocational rehabilitation. They also develop an operational computerized model to produce cost-benefit estimates for different population groups of rehabilitants.

Barsby, Steve L. COST-BENEFIT ANALYSIS AND MANPOWER PROGRAMS. Lexington, Mass.: Lexington Books, 1972. 180 p.

An initial chapter briefly surveys some of the major thinking in this field, and highlights findings from Bruce Davie's cost-benefit survey of vocational education programs. Other chapters report on the major findings of those who studied secondary school and post-secondary school vocational education, institutional out-of-school retraining, and other manpower program approaches.

Berkley, George. "Municipal Garages in Boston: A Cost-Benefit Analysis." TRAFFIC QUARTERLY 19 (April 1965): 213-28.

Then chairman of Boston's finance commission, the author summarizes the research in a case study quite useful for introducing this field of inquiry. The study indicated that the garages were being overmonopolized by all-day parkers; the garages were

causing more congestion than they were alleviating; and the
amount of profit to retailers attributable to the garages was dis-
proportionate to the costs involved.

Bogosian, Theodore; Harrity, Deborah; and Lynn, Laurence E., Jr. THE CEN-
TRAL UTAH PROJECT. Kennedy School of Government. Boston: Intercollegiate Case Clearing House, 1976. Case A (C15-76-120): 28 p.; case B (C15-
76-121): 35 p.; Lynn Memorandum Case (C15-76-121A): 5 p.

> These materials provide extraordinary insight into a policy de-
> cision concerning a key issue confronting the U.S. Department
> of Interior in 1973. Case A, for example, reproduces the rele-
> vant policy memoranda within the department, including the
> "Program Decision Option Document" examining the stop, delay,
> and continue construction alternatives. Environmental impact
> statements require the evaluation of alternatives as a major focus
> of their analyses, and, in doing so, carry on the cost-benefit
> traditions of the natural resources field. These cases place this
> tradition into perspective within the overall discipline of policy
> analysis. There are also rich readings on the politics, economics,
> and history of the issue, which flesh out the realities of the
> context confronting the decision makers. Assistant Secretary
> Lynn's recommendations complete the set of available case ma-
> terials.

Bogosian, Theodore; Mates, William; and Lynn, Laurence E., Jr. AUTOMO-
BILE EMISSIONS CONTROL: THE SULFATES PROBLEM. Cambridge, Mass.:
Kennedy School of Government, Harvard University, 1975. Case A (C95-76-
077): 27 p.; case B (C15-76-078): 30 p.; sequel case (C15-76-078S): 10 p.

> The U.S. Environmental Protection Agency is confronted with
> responsibility for enforcement of Clear Air Act amendments con-
> taining new, explicit, and strict standards for the control of
> atmospheric pollutants in automobile exhaust. Case A discusses
> implementation considerations: quality control; health standards;
> and emission control requirements; energy; emission control tech-
> nology; lead time; fuel additives; and nitrogen oxide measure-
> ment problems. Case B expands upon an EPA issue paper en-
> titled "Estimated Public Health Impact As a Result of Equipping
> Light-Duty Motor Vehicles with Oxidation Catalysts." The se-
> quel details the decision and the criticism in response to it.

Borus, Michael E. "A Benefit-Cost Analysis of the Economic Effectiveness of
Retraining the Unemployed." YALE ECONOMIC ESSAYS 4 (1964): 370-429.

> This essay, summarizing a dissertation, is based on interview
> data gathered from 373 Connecticut retrainees. Benefits are de-
> rived from multiple regression analyses comparing the experience
> of retrainees with the experience of those who did not enter or
> did not complete the program. Workers who utilized their re-

training skills were found to have substantially improved employment records, and the program was interpreted as operating in areas where retraining would not otherwise occur, even though the gains to the economy would be significant. Since the external effects of retraining yield high social benefits when private benefits may be quite low, the author feels that governmental assumption of the costs of the program is proper and necessary.

_____, ed. EVALUATING THE IMPACT OF MANPOWER PROGRAMS. Proceedings of a conference conducted 15-17 June 1971 at the Center for Human Research, Ohio State University. Lexington, Mass.: D.C. Heath and Co., 1972. 280 p.

Emphases among the twenty collected papers include: discussion of secondary effects, such as displacement of other workers; the multiprogram evaluation approach initiated by DOL and OEO; survey instrument design considerations; control group selection; and noneconomic impact.

Borus, Michael E.; Brennan, John P.; and Rosen, Sidney. "A Benefit-Cost Analysis of the Neighborhood Youth Corps; The Out-of-School Program in Indiana." JOURNAL OF HUMAN RESOURCES 5 (Winter 1970): 130-59.

The article describes a study of cost data and regression analyses of both participant and eligible nonparticipant earnings in five urban areas of Indiana. The program is viewed as much more than an "aging vat" for youth, since the earnings gain was substantial for males. The researchers recommend that early dropouts be encouraged to remain in the program as long as possible.

Carroll, Stephen J., and Pascal, Anthony H. A SYSTEMS ANALYTIC APPROACH TO THE EMPLOYMENT PROBLEMS OF DISADVANTAGED YOUTH. Report P-4045. Santa Monica, Calif.: Rand Corp., March 1969. 25 p.

The authors view the problem in terms of reduction in the inequalities of lifetime economic performance of disadvantaged youth. They lay out a conceptual model of the youth employment situation through a set of simultaneous equations to predict the economic prospects for an individual on the basis of his or her experiences, tastes, abilities, perceptions, and opportunities. Equations are developed to represent lifetime earnings, youth behavior, perceptions and anticipations, the returns from alternative activities, and labor market opportunities. The essential output of the model is the "activity path," viewed as the true indicator of economic opportunity in any long-run sense.

Christenson, Charles. DISEASE CONTROL PROGRAMS (A). Boston: Intercollegiate Case Clearing House, 1967. Case 9-112-007: 19 p.; teaching note 5-112-077: 4 p.

This Civil Service Commission case is a classic example of cost-benefit analysis, representing a series of federal staff analyses covering a variety of health program areas. In fact, the "disease" analyzed is fatalities resulting from motorcycle accidents. Valuation of human life is a significant aspect of the analysis.

Cohn, Edwin J. "Assessing the Costs and Benefits of Anti-Malaria Programs: The Indian Experience." AMERICAN JOURNAL OF PUBLIC HEALTH 63 (December 1973): 1086-96.

Average unit costs in the attack and consolidation stages are developed. Control and eradication campaign costs are compared. Reduced mortality, increased fertility, and reduced morbidity are defined as direct benefits. Eradication, argues the author, is similar in its cost implications to a control approach. Demographic impact should be a key evaluative consideration.

Collignon, Frederick C. A WORKING OUTLINE FOR COST-BENEFIT ANALYSIS OF VOCATIONAL REHABILITATION PROGRAMS. Working paper 174/RS004. Berkeley: University of California, Institute of Urban and Regional Development, November 1971. 41 p.

This document is an outline laying out the institute's cost-benefit research in the area of rehabilitation programming. It discusses their approach to costs: variable, fixed program, and program carry-over costs; foregone earnings; costs borne by other agencies, the individual, and his family; and repeater costs. Paid employment earnings are discussed in terms of increased earnings capabilities, lifetime projections, adjustments for secular gains in productivity, adjustments for differential mortality rates, costs required after closure to sustain employment, and displacement of others from jobs. Finally, there is a discussion of the selection of client subpopulations for disaggregated cost-benefit estimates.

Conley, Ronald W. "A Benefit-Cost Analysis of the Vocational Rehabilitation Program." JOURNAL OF HUMAN RESOURCES 4 (Spring 1969): 226-52.

In this pivotal article, the author concludes that from the standpoint of economic efficiency, it may be as desirable to rehabilitate the less productive disabled as their more productive counterparts. The variations in increased earnings due to rehabilitation were much less significant for those with the highest earnings at both acceptance and closure--white, male, well-educated, married and supporting children and suffering from orthopedic difficulties. However, estimations of increased lifetime earnings per case service dollar led the author to target the nonwhite, uneducated, unmarried, middle-aged, and severely disabled potential participants.

Dittenhofer, Martin A.; Wallace, William A.; and Axelrod, Donald. POLICE
TAKE-HOME PATROL PLAN. Rensselaer Polytechnic Institute and State University
of New York at Albany. Boston: Intercollegiate Case Clearing House, 1977. Case
9-378-510: 31 p.; teaching note 5-378-511: 19 p.

> Montgomery County, Maryland, police officers are allowed to
> use their patrol cars for personal transportation in exchange for
> responding to any calls for aid, as well as any crimes or emer-
> gencies they may encounter. The case requires a decision as
> to whether this program should be continued, expanded, or can-
> celled.

Dodson, Richard, and Cole, Charles B. AN INTRODUCTION TO COST
BENEFIT ANALYSIS OF THE VOCATIONAL REHABILITATION PROGRAM: A
MODEL FOR USE BY STATE AGENCIES. Working paper 192/RS015. Berkeley:
University of California, Institute of Urban and Regional Development, October
1972. 35 p.

> After briefly introducing the overall approach, the authors de-
> tail the model developed for vocational rehabilitation. They
> propose a definition of program costs in terms of both case ser-
> vice and overhead items, and suggest inclusion of costs borne
> by other agencies, repeater costs, foregone output, and research,
> demonstration and training costs, but exclusion of carryover and
> maintenance costs. Benefits include increase in earnings and
> increase in nonpaid output, such as homemaking and other non-
> paid work.

Fischoff, Baruch. "Cost Benefit Analysis and the Art of Motorcycle Maintenance."
POLICY SCIENCES 8 (June 1977): 177-202.

> The article discusses the approach in terms of its rationality,
> acceptability for decision-making purposes, problems in appli-
> cation, and potential misuse. For example, the author examines
> the question of the distribution of costs and benefits to different
> groups. Risk assessments are examined in terms of unanticipated
> human errors and changes in the environment, overconfidence in
> scientific and technical knowledge, and the failure to see the
> surrounding systems operating as a whole. Valuation of life and
> "societal gambles" are also scrutinized.

Forbes, Roy H. "Cost-Effectiveness Analysis: Primer and Guidelines." EDU-
CATIONAL TECHNOLOGY 14 (March 1974): 21-27.

> The author argues that four elements are essential to the analysis,
> and defines these elements at length: program descriptions, stu-
> dent characteristics, effectiveness measures, and costs. The ar-
> ticle describes costs as "capital" or "operating," "direct" or
> "indirect," "individual" versus "society," and "measurable"
> versus "nonmeasurable." It goes on to describe how to collect
> data and then establish and interpret ratio comparisons.

Frost, Michael J. HOW TO USE COST BENEFIT ANALYSIS IN PROJECT APPRAISAL. New York: John Wiley and Sons, 1975. 202 p.

> This British consultant presents a series of European case studies on the application of and the context surrounding the technique. He adds his own thinking and recommendations on how others might further apply the analysis.

Goldman, Thomas, ed. COST-EFFECTIVENESS ANALYSIS: NEW APPROACHES IN DECISIONMAKING. New York: Praeger Publishers, 1967. 231 p.

> This Washington Operations Research Council symposium features an introductory piece by Edward Quade and an article by William Niskanen on defense effectiveness measures. Harry Hatry discusses cost issues--cost estimating relationships, the treatment of uncertainty, and measures for static as well as time-phased analyses. There are also pieces by William Capron on domestic programs generally, John Kain on transportation, and Stanley Besen, Alan Fechter, and Anthony Fisher on the poverty program.

Goldschmidt, Peter G. "A Cost-Effectiveness Model for Evaluating Health Care Programs: Application To Drug Abuse Treatment." INQUIRY 13 (March 1976): 29-47.

> After constructing a cost-effectiveness model for health and social service programs, the author applies the approach to drug treatment programs. Treatment modalities are defined in terms of the type of drugs or medication provided, the type of facility, and the scheduled length of treatment. Effectiveness data was derived from 1,241 interviews with past and present patients in ten programs across the country. It pertained to reduced drug use, crime committed by users, and user rehabilitation, particularly in terms of job readiness. Total program effectiveness was found to be approximately equal between the therapeutic community and the methadone maintenance programs evaluated. However, neither type of program retains more than half of its patients in treatment for more than six months, despite their philosophic commitments to extended treatment.

Goldstein, Harvey. COST-BENEFIT AND COST-EFFECTIVENESS ANALYSIS. Policy-Program Analysis and Evaluation Techniques. Package 6, Module 5. Washington, D.C.: Urban Management Curriculum Development Project, National Training and Development Service, 1977. 53 p.

> A brief summary piece explaining the approach is coupled with a series of exercises (e.g., present value techniques and "excess" benefit) and case studies (a state highway by-pass, a rapid transit technology demonstration, institutional manpower training versus on-the-job training, library journal subscription questions).

Goldstein, Roberta. COST/OUTPUT ANALYSIS OF ALTERNATIVE PROCEDURES
FOR A HOSPITAL SURVEILLANCE PROGRAM. Report R789-NYC. Santa
Monica, Calif.: Rand Corp., August 1971. 38 p.

In this New York City Rand Institute analysis, New York's
Bureau of Maternity Services and Family Planning is responsible
for the surveillance of all proprietary, voluntary, and municipal facilities that provide maternity, newborn, family planning,
and abortion services. Working from a fixed budget, five alternative procedures are evaluated according to estimates of
their projected costs and service output levels. Alternative
procedures include the substitution of outline reports for narrative reports, changes in the frequency of the visits, and the
uitlization of one-physician surveys at proprietary hospitals.

Gray, Charles M.; Conover, C. Johnston; and Hennessey, Timothy M. "Cost
Effectiveness of Residential Community Corrections: An Analytical Prototype."
EVALUATION QUARTERLY 2 (August 1978): 375-400.

This study reviews the relative cost effectiveness of community
corrections, probation, and incarceration as alternative means
of treating convicted offenders. The findings indicate that, for
clients who have never been institutionalized, under five measures of recidivism, probation appears to be more cost effective
than community-based residential treatment. The authors discuss
new policy options suggested by the analysis, such as doubling
client-staff ratios in the more expensive institutions, reduction
of the length of stay in the least cost-effective alternatives,
and the operation of facilities at 90 percent capacity.

Haggart, Sue A. INCREASING THE EFFECTIVE USE OF ANALYSIS THROUGH
PROGRAM-ORIENTED MANAGEMENT. Santa Monica, Calif.: Rand Corp.,
April 1972. 11 p. Paperbound.

It is a mistake to try to select a "best" English course in cost-
effectiveness terms, rather than employing analytic techniques to
focus on such aspects as method, resource use, and outcomes.
The author argues for the use of analysis to further educational
goals through program-structure-based planning rather than only
through logistical thinking.

Hannan, Timothy H. "The Benefits and Costs of Methadone Maintenance."
PUBLIC POLICY 24 (Spring 1976): 197-226.

In this example of the ground-breaking work of the author in
this field, benefits are described in terms of decreases in criminal
justice expenditures, of medical expenditures for narcotic-related
illnesses, of direct expenditures on heroin, and of an increase in
legal earnings. New York City's Methadone Maintenance Treatment Program patients provide the data for the analysis. The
author finds that benefits exceed costs, most likely by a very

wide margin, but that this conclusion should be considered within a context in which other factors are weighed: legal sanctions against heroin use; alternative modalities; and the inappropriateness of methadone for those with multiple addictions, and other nonparticipants.

Hansen, W. Lee, and Weisbrod, Burton A. THE DISTRIBUTION OF COSTS AND DIRECT BENEFITS OF PUBLIC HIGHER EDUCATION: THE CASE OF CALIFORNIA. Reprint 36. Madison: University of Wisconsin, Institute for Research on Poverty, 1969. 17 p.

> Publicly subsidized higher education is found to promote greater rather than lesser inequality among people of various social and economic backgrounds, by making available substantial subsidies that lower income families are either not eligible for, or cannot make use of, because of other conditions or constraints associated with their income position. Changing the system might involve overhauling pricing, realigning taxes, or broadening eligibility. This paper and the authors' further work on this subject provide clear representative examples of the approach economists take in analyzing the allocation of program benefits.

Harberger, Arnold, and Wisecarver, Daniel, eds. BENEFIT COST ANALYSIS, 1971. Chicago: Aldine-Atherton, 1972. 485 p.

> Articles of special importance in this anthology include the measurement of the value of life; cost-benefit analysis of polio; mass radiography for detecting tuberculosis; Upward-Bound; junior colleges; Rand housing evaluation; the Mexico City airport; the third London airport; and a travel-cost, consumer-surplus benefits estimation for recreation facility planning purposes.

Hardin, Einar, and Borus, Michael E. THE ECONOMIC BENEFITS AND COSTS OF RETRAINING. Lexington, Mass.: D.C. Heath and Co., 1971. 235 p.

> This Department of Labor study reviewed institutional and occupationally oriented programs in Michigan. It employed three economic criteria: output of the nation; disposable income of the trainee; and the government budget. The training was not found to be self-supporting, and the gain in annual earnings from taking the training was found to decline the longer one stayed in the program.

Haveman, Robert M., with Wisecarver, Daniel, eds. BENEFIT-COST AND POLICY ANALYSIS, 1973. Chicago: Aldine Publishing Co., 1974. 524 p.

> Highlights include Donald Shoup on alternative experimental allocations of police resources in Los Angeles; Haveman, Irene Lurie, and Thad Mirer on an earnings supplementation plan as an income-transfer strategy; Edgar Browning's contrasting of a

negative income tax with a negative wage tax; Leonard Weiss's cost-benefit study of antitrust prosecutions; Martin Feldstein's view of the American family as overinsured for health protection; Richard Zeckhauser on catastrophic illness; and John Holahan's Urban Institute evaluation of corrections reform at Project Crossroads.

Hinrichs, Harley H., and Taylor, Graeme M., eds. SYSTEMATIC ANALYSIS: A PRIMER ON BENEFIT-COST ANALYSIS AND PROGRAM EVALUATION. Pacific Palisades, Calif.: Goodyear Publishing Co., 1972. 152 p.

The editor's provide a casebook of cost-benefit exercises, including the widely used Dade County swimming opportunities case. Other cases presented for possible analysis include a work-study program for mentally retarded children; manpower planning for the early childhood handicapped; and a bombs versus missiles Air Force problem. Also included are examples of completed cost-benefit analysis: court delays; small-site industrial renewal; and fireboat deployment. Finally, the authors add a brief introduction to issue analysis and Donald Schon's article on "the blindness system."

Hughes, James W., ed. METHODS OF HOUSING ANALYSIS: TECHNIQUES AND CASE STUDIES. New Brunswick, N.J.: Center for Urban Policy Research, Rutgers University, 1977. 551 p.

This casebook lays out methods of calculating housing investment costs and benefits. Discounted cash-flow internal rate of return analysis is presented, showing how present value considerations, depreciation and tax impact, and the projection of capital gains at resale can all be used to contrast alternative projects. Also presented is the approach applied by the Rutgers staff to the cost-revenue trade-offs confronted by communities reviewing new housing development possibilities.

Kent, James; Wallace, William A.; and Axelrod, Donald. RESERVOIR FOR DECATUR. Rensselaer Polytechnic Institute and State University of New York at Albany. Boston: Intercollegiate Case Clearing House, n.d. Case 9-378-524: 44 p.; teaching note 5-378-525: 7 p.

The Oakley Reservoir proposal, forty years old, of the Army Corps of Engineers in proposed as a subject for state legislative cost-benefit analysis. Needs, costs, and levels of environmental awareness have all changed and require reappraisal.

Klarman, Herbert E. "Present Status of Cost-Benefit Analysis in the Health Field." AMERICAN JOURNAL OF PUBLIC HEALTH 57 (November 1967): 1948-53.

The writer describes three categories of benefits: savings in the use of health resources; gains in economic output; and satisfactions

from better health. He discusses the special difficulties associated with defining the "costs" of diseases.

Law, Warren A., and Taylor, Graeme M. OFFICE OF ECONOMIC OP-
PORTUNITY (A). Boston: Intercollegiate Case Clearing House, 1967. Case
9-112-050: 33 p.; teaching notes 5-112-074: 5 p.; and 5-176-210: 8 p.

This is the classic case containing selections of readings reflec-
ting alternative approaches to evaluating the costs and benefits
of antipoverty programs. Developed as one of the Civil Service
Commission series of cases, it emphasizes the difficulties in
measuring benefits. Three separate internal agency papers reviewing the success of the Job Corps are utilized.

Levin, Henry M. COST-EFFECTIVENESS ANALYSIS IN EVALUATION RESEARCH.
Stanford, Calif.: Stanford Evaluation Consortium, March 1974. 81 p.

In this clearly written basic text, costs are discussed in terms
of social sacrifices (opportunity costs) as well as in terms of
financial outlays. Illustrative cost "ingredients" worksheets include listings for components such as foregone client earnings.
Effectiveness is examined in terms of the time pattern of results
measures for multiple outcomes, and the distribution of effects
among different populations.

Levine, Abraham S. "Cost-Benefit Analysis and Social Welfare: An Explora-
tion of Possible Applications." WELFARE IN REVIEW 4 (February 1966): 1-11.

This article is an example of some of the earliest advocacy of
the approach in the social welfare field. The author, for example, argues strongly for sharpened definition of intervention
goals. He reviews the first Borus manpower study and suggests
the need for cost-benefit analysis of both local demonstration
projects and national income maintenance strategies.

_____. "Evaluating Program Effectiveness and Efficiency: Rationale and De-
scription of Research in Progress." WELFARE IN REVIEW 5 (February 1967):
1-11.

This clearly written explanatory piece for the social welfare
field discusses such questions as how outputs differ from benefits
and how program models should be designed. The author discusses research then underway evaluating the Bernalillo County
Welfare Department's AFDC program, and day care personnel
training in Los Angeles.

_____. "Rehabilitating Disabled Welfare Recipients: A Cost-Benefit Analysis."
WELFARE IN REVIEW 6 (September-October 1968): 14-18.

The author presents an analysis which he views as simple, because the economic results are considerably in excess of the

cost, and all that is necessary is to show that the program is worthwhile. An integrated method of rehabilitating carefully selected disabled public assistance recipients is studied.

Lichfield, Nathaniel. "Cost-Benefit Analysis in City Planning." JOURNAL OF THE AMERICAN INSTITUTE OF PLANNERS 26 (November 1970): 273-79.

This article was a major influence in encouraging urban planners to apply cost-benefit analysis to city planning. A welfare test of the cost-benefit variety is proposed as a means of rationalizing planning practice and improving the quality of decisions. Planning departments are defined as "supra-investment agencies." The authors propose that each project should be measured in terms of social accounts.

Luft, Harold S. "Benefit-Cost Analysis and Public Policy Implementation: From Normative to Positive Analysis." PUBLIC POLICY 24 (Fall 1976): 437-62.

The author focuses on implementation phases of projects and policies: whether and how the project will be done. Predictive analysis is proposed to determine whether a project should be done (whether it would be a social improvement); the likelihood of whether it will be done (reviewed from the perspective of each decision maker or group which might influence the project's success); and the alternative ways of getting it done (e.g., special incentives to improve the likelihood of success). A case study is presented which describes the application of this approach to the program design of ambulatory surgery centers.

Maass, Arthur. "Benefit Cost Analysis: Its Relevance to Public Investment Decisions." QUARTERLY JOURNAL OF ECONOMICS 80 (May 1966): 208-26.

The author recognizes that the technique tends to focus practitioners on the efficiency objective, but urges agencies to at least work with two-term objective functions. He challenges other cost-benefit economists to review their assumptions concerning consumers' sovereignty and their historical indifference to the distribution of programmatic benefits.

McBride, Howard J. "Benefit-Cost Analysis and Local Government Decision-Making." GOVERNMENTAL FINANCE 4 (February 1975): 31-34.

The author argues that local governments will limit their ability to determine policy if they fail to employ the technique. They will not be able to compare private versus public expenditures, or evaluate all of the alternative solutions to a problem. Also, they might eliminate worthy projects by too rigid adherence to budget constraints, or take on projects based upon their urgency without due regard to their cost.

Maidlow, Spencer T., and Berman, Howard. "The Economics of Heroin Treatment." AMERICAN JOURNAL OF PUBLIC HEALTH 62 (October 1972): 1397-1406.

>Cost-benefit analysis is employed to contrast therapeutic communities with methadone programs as alternative resolutions of the heroin addiction problem, after British system and long-term institutionalization alternatives are discarded. Criteria include average length of stay, direct cost per addict per year, program success rate, and total unadjusted cost to graduate one addict. Appendixes detail the basis for the cost and benefit matrix figures.

Marcus, William B., and Lynn, Laurence E., Jr. HIGH MOUNTAIN SHEEP DAM. Cambridge, Mass.: Kennedy School of Government, 1976. Basic Case C15-75-049: 22 p.; sequel C15-75-049S: 2 p.

>Hells Canyon possesses great scenic value and the potential for being the best remaining hydroelectric site in the coterminous United States. The case poses the issue of the canyon's future, which confronted the staff of the Federal Power Commission. The case requires analysis of the present value of project costs, comparisons between hydroelectric and thermal cost alternatives, determination of the annual capacity benefit, and projections of short-run, off-peak fuel savings benefits.

_____. LOCKS AND DAM 26. Cambridge, Mass.: Kennedy School of Government, 1976. (A) Case C15-76-095: 29.; (B) case C15-76-096: 50 p.; (C) case and exercise answer sheet C15-76-097: 34 p.

>The (A) case details the background of the Army Corps of Engineers, and the economic criteria it employs in evaluating the feasibility of projects. The (B) case lays out the issue concerning replacement of the Alton facilities. It discusses environmental concerns, railroad opposition, air pollution and energy efficiency considerations, accidents and spills, dredging, turbidity and bank erosion questions, and matters of development and flood protection. The (C) case provides the data needed to conduct a cost-benefit analysis of the economic feasibility of the project.

_____. NOTE ON BENEFIT-COST ANALYSIS. Case N15-76-110. Cambridge, Mass.: Kennedy School of Government, 1976. 16 p.

>This brief note summarizes the economics literature on this subject for lay readers. It discusses the underlying theories, measurement (shadow prices, externalities and public goods, consumers' surplus, and systemwide effects), the discount rate and project life, and the use of the technique for investment purposes.

Marshall, Eliot. "Anatomy of Health Care Costs: CAT Fever." NEW RE-PUBLIC, 16 April 1977, pp. 11-15.

> In this article in his series on health care cost containment issues, the author discusses the politics surrounding the question of whether the CAT's (Computerized Axial Tomographic Scanner) benefits to society are worth the cost. The author describes the question as an example of a professional determination deciding what kind of service is a luxury and what is standard. Problems in the pricing and use of the CAT scanner are detailed.

Max, Laurence, and Downs, Thomas. DECENTRALIZED DELINQUENCY SERVICES IN MICHIGAN: DIFFERENTIAL PLACEMENT AND ITS IMPACT ON PROGRAM EFFECTIVENESS AND COST-EFFECTIVENESS. Studies in Welfare Policy, no. 4. Lansing: Michigan Department of Social Services, Evaluation and Analysis Division, March 1975. 160 p.

> This study indicates that a special intake center approach was most instrumental in enabling aggressive hard-to-place youth obtain less structured and noninstitutional placements which were at least as effective, and a bit more cost effective than placements made by the regular intake office. Although institutions (having compulsory skill attainment programs, with skill attainment a measure of effectiveness) were found to be slightly more effective than community placements, the higher cost of institutionalization made that form of care less cost effective than community care.

Mishan, Edward J. COST-BENEFIT ANALYSIS. New York: Praeger Publishers, 1976. 454 p.

> The approach is discussed in terms of a variety of different questions: the choice of investment criteria, opportunity cost in regard to shadow prices for labor, selection of discount rates, valuation of time, and market-based estimates of pollution damage.

_____. ECONOMICS FOR SOCIAL DECISIONS: ELEMENTS OF COST-BENEFIT ANALYSIS. New York: Praeger Publishers, 1973. 151 p.

> The author addresses such fundamental issues as the measurement of consumers' surplus, the measurement of rent, the economic cost of unemployed factors, transfer payments, shadow prices, the evaluation of accidents and death, and discounted present value versus the internal rate of return.

Munch, Patricia. COSTS AND BENEFITS OF THE TORT SYSTEM IF VIEWED AS A COMPENSATION SYSTEM. Paper P-5921. Santa Monica, Calif.: Rand Corp., June 1977. 95 p.

> In this paper prepared for the California Citizens' Commission on

Tort Reform, the author examines the insurance costs of the tort liability system, the allocation of the premium dollar between injured claimants, claimant and defense litigation costs, and insurance overhead. In all the tort lines, there appears to be a pattern of overcompensation in cases with relatively low economic loss, and undercompensation in cases with relatively large reported economic loss.

National Academy of Sciences. Institute of Medicine. A POLICY STATEMENT: COMPUTED TOMOGRAPHIC SCANNING. Washington, D.C.: April 1977. 54 p.

This report provides Blue Cross with the recommendations of an institute committee on the issues of efficacy, planning policy, utilization, costs and charges, and information and evaluation needs. The question is described as a watershed for policy decisions about appropriate distribution and use of costly medical technologies. The report urges a low rate of professional charges, state regulation through the certificate-of-need process, and acceptance as criteria of efficacy of the usual standards of clinical practice.

Nelson, Carl W. "Cost-Benefit Analysis and Alternatives to Incarceration." FEDERAL PROBATION 39 (December 1975): 467-76.

This article presents the classification logic which the Correctional Economics Center employs in its analyses. Both costs and benefits are organized around three perspectives: governmental (affecting local, state, and federal funds flow), social (affecting national income or accumulated wealth), and individual (affecting the personal or family income of the convicted criminal).

Niskanen, William, and Wisecarver, Daniel, eds. BENEFIT-COST AND POLICY ANALYSIS 1972. Chicago: Aldine Publishing Co., 1973. 535 p.

This volume in the Aldine series begins with a debate on the legitimacy of policy analysis between Laurence Tribe and Alan Williams. Herman Van der Tak and Arandarup Ray describe the consumer-surplus concept in their piece on the economic benefits of road transport projects. Jon H. Goldstein criticizes manpower program evaluations for overestimating benefits by basing estimates on immediate post-training income.

Noble, John M., Jr. "The Limits of Cost-Benefit Analysis as a Guide to Priority-Setting in Rehabilitation." EVALUATION QUARTERLY 1 (August 1977): 347-80.

The article argues that eighteen previous cost-benefit studies in the field have contributed little to the resource allocation debate on alternative kinds and amounts of investments. These studies have shown greater rates of return for investments in some kinds of disabled people over others, but the author claims that they are extremely sensitive to untested underlying assumptions, and involve overly simplistic forecasting of future earnings of rehabilitants.

Petersen, Robert L. "The Use and Misuse of Cost Effectiveness." AIR UNIVERSITY REVIEW 17 (March–April 1966): 81–84.

In comparing competitive missile and aircraft system alternatives, the author finds his conclusion is dependent upon the values to be placed on human life, and on estimation of the likelihood of general nuclear war. The usefulness of the approach is in the highlighting of the sensitivity of conclusions to the various factors involved in the problem. The article is interesting in its demonstration of the willingness of defense department policy analysts to quantify for decision-making purposes extraordinary behavioral and value assumptions. The application of analytic techniques to domestic policies would meet far more resistance in these areas.

Plant, Jeremy F.; Wallace, William A.; and Axelrod, Donald. TITLE IV-D PROGRAM IN NEW YORK STATE: A CASE STUDY IN PROGRAM MANAGEMENT. Rensselaer Polytechnic Institute and State University of New York at Albany. Boston: Intercollegiate Case Clearing House, 1977. Case 9-378-504: 25 p.; teaching note 5-378-505: 7 p.

The performance goals for a county's IV-D Aid to Families Dependent Children parent locator program are the subject of this case. Should the county agency seek the greatest financial return (in collected court-ordered child support payments) for each invested program dollar, or alternatively should it seek to locate as many parents as possible regardless of whether they will be able to make the payments?

Potter, Alan; Binner, Paul R.; and Halpern, Joseph. "Strategies for Resource Allocation: A Cost-Benefit Approach to Program Management." Paper presented at the Annual Meeting of the Southern Regional Conference on Mental Health Statistics, New Orleans, 3–6 October 1976. Denver: Fort Logan Mental Health Center, 1976. 17 p.

Using output value analysis, the authors determined that rapid increases in benefits which occurred initially were followed by much smaller incremental gains. They discuss the point of diminishing returns as a minimum funding level, except for experimental programs, in which patients are treated to the limit of the state of the art.

Prest, Alan R., and Turvey, Ralph. "Cost-Benefit Analysis: A Survey." ECONOMIC JOURNAL 75 (December 1965): 683–735.

This survey is the most complete review of the literature up until 1965. It succinctly presents general principles-enumeration (ex-

ternalities, secondary benefits), valuation (relevant prices, non-
marginal changes, market imperfections, taxes and controls, unemployment, collective goods, intangibles), and choice of the
interest rate (social time preference rate, social opportunity
cost rate, adjustment for uncertainty), and constraints (distributional, budgetary). There is also a then-current summary of
research undertaken in the different service-delivery areas.

Price, Willard T.; Wallace, William A.; and Axelrod, Donald. REVERSIBLE
LANE SIGNALIZATION. Rensselaer Polytechnic Institute and State University
of New York at Albany. Boston: Intercollegiate Case Clearing House, Case
9-178-680: 30 p.; teaching note 9-178-681: 25 p.

The Tucson city manager evaluates a reversible lane configura-
tion on one of its busiest streets and the overhead electronic
equipment used to control traffic there, as a method of relieving
rush hour traffic congestion. An alternative option, employing
work crews and traffic cones, is contrasted in terms of cost and
performance criteria.

Quinn, Michael, and Mendelson, Robert. THE FEASIBILITY OF LEAD PAINT
REMOVAL IN ST. LOUIS RENTAL HOUSING. Edwardsville: Center for Urban
and Environmental Research and Services, Southern Illinois University, June 1978.
40 p. Paperbound.

The authors analyze data demonstrating the cost and feasibility
trade-offs involved in lead paint poisoning treatment programs.
The basis for defining technical treatment standards is also examined.

Rhoads, Steven E. "How Much Should We Spend to Save a Life?" PUBLIC
INTEREST 51 (Spring 1978): 74-92.

The writer details the background of the debate over measurement of this cost-benefit issue, and clearly describes both the
"discounted future earnings" and "willingness-to-pay" approaches.
Arguments are accompanied by a review of the discussions among
philosophers, economists, and theologians about the resource allocation question involving lifesaving therapy--should the most
deserving be saved, or should everyone be treated equally?

Rudolph, Claire S.; Wallace, William A.; and Axelrod, Donald. IMPLEMENT-
ING CHAP IN MOHAWK COUNTY. Rensselaer Polytechnic Institute and State
University of New York at Albany. Boston: Intercollegiate Case Clearing
House, 1978. Case 9-378-502: 7 p.; teaching note 5-378-503: 7 p.

A Mohawk County program to provide regular health care to
Medicaid-eligible children was cited for noncompliance with
state regulations. With little money for additional staffing,
alternative staffing patterns must be evaluated according to their
projected cost and performance.

Singer, Max. "How To Reduce Risks Rationally." PUBLIC INTEREST 51 (Spring 1978): 93-112.

> The author addresses lifesaving policy alternatives of two classes: postponing death from old age and preventing early death. He lays out a classification of hazards: currently identifiable causes of death (basically accidents); insidious contaminants and environmentally caused diseases; smoking; and potential population destroyers. He also discusses the costs of changing victim behavior, trading one risk for another (e.g., electricity for nuclear reactors), spending money, preventing progress, and "being smarter."

Smolensky, Eugene, and Gomery, J. Douglas. EFFICIENCY AND EQUITY BENEFITS FROM THE FEDERAL HOUSING PROGRAM IN 1965. Reprint 88. Madison: University of Wisconsin, Institute for Research on Poverty, 1973. 39 p.

> By utilizing the resource cost approach for measuring subsidy, the authors find a benefit which is very small when compared to costs. If the goal of the program is viewed in output maximization terms--the number of families voluntarily moving from substandard to standard units--vouchers are proposed as a preferable alternative. Analysis of the requirements for horizontal equity suggests a need for a supplementary program to aid the nonurban poor.

Solomon, Arthur P. THE COST EFFECTIVENESS OF SUBSIDIZED HOUSING. Working paper 5. Cambridge, Mass.: Joint Center for Urban Studies, February 1972. 40 p.

> The author examines conventional and turnkey public housing, leased public housing, and rent supplements. He asks three questions. What is the most cost-effective method of providing low-income families with shelter? What proportion of the total cost is subsidized by the government, and what proportion reaches the tenant (as opposed to administrative overhead)? What is the value of foregone government revenue from tax concessions? The leasing of existing units is found to be more cost effective than any rehabilitation or new construction strategy.

Somers, Gerald G., and Stromsdorfer, Ernst W. A COST EFFECTIVENESS STUDY OF THE IN-SCHOOL AND SUMMER NEIGHBORHOOD YOUTH CORPS. Madison: University of Wisconsin, Industrial Relations Research Institute, July 1970. 436 p.

> A national evaluation was undertaken of this program to determine whether, in fact, it reduced the high school dropout rate, improved the quality of students' educational experience, and helped to provide skills of use in the job market. While overall the program failed to affect dropout rates, black participants

were 8.2 percent more likely to graduate than their control
group counterparts. Participants' earnings were enhanced by
the encouragement they received to participate in the labor
force.

Squire, Lyn, and Van der Tak, Herman G. ECONOMIC ANALYSIS OF PROJ-
ECTS. Baltimore: Johns Hopkins University Press, 1975. 153 p.

This study focuses on the World Bank's need to decide whether
or not to loan developing countries the funds for specific projects. While much of the book discusses the theory of shadow
prices and the empirical estimation of shadow prices, the authors also detail their process of weighing criteria within a
single aggregate index in order to come to decisions.

Sternlieb, George; Roistacher, Elizabeth; and Hughes, James W. TAX SUB-
SIDIES AND HOUSING INVESTMENT: A FISCAL COST-BENEFIT ANALYSIS.
New Brunswick, N.J.: Transaction Books, 1976. 86 p.

This study attempts to place the housing subsidy and investment
programs in New York City into a cost-benefit perspective.
In particular, private housing market intervention strategies are
reviewed in terms of their contribution to the production of low-
and middle-income units. The Economic Development Council
of New York City sponsored this research, which also provides
an operational quantitative model to analyze the effects of
specific mechanisms designed to stimulate the local housing
system.

Taylor, Graeme M. SWIMMING POOLS. George Washington University.
Boston: Intercollegiate Case Clearing House, 1968. Case 9-113-023. 3 p.;
teaching note 5-113-151: 28 p.

This case, developed as part of the Planning Programming Budgetary Systems 5-5-5 program, presents a simple decision involving the selection of the best way to serve model cities residents' needs. The teaching note includes Dade County's actual
program analysis and a note by the author explaining present
value techniques.

Teitz, Michael B. COST EFFECTIVENESS: A SYSTEMS APPROACH TO THE
ANALYSIS OF URBAN SERVICES. Reprint 39. Berkeley: University of California, Institute of Urban and Regional Development, 1968. 8 p.

Lacking a price mechanism, government agencies are advised to
employ this approach which does not necessarily describe output
in dollar terms. The author differentiates between technical
performance and generalized system standards in his discussion
of the need to be selective in defining measurements.

Therkildsen, Paul, and Reno, Philip. "Cost-Benefit Evaluation of the Bernalillo County Work Experience Project." WELFARE IN REVIEW 6 (March–April 1968): 1–12.

> This study analyzes the project as a model for manpower training program evaluation. The article discusses topics such as the target population, tangible versus intangible costs and benefits, labor market factors, the distribution of costs and benefits, and financial disincentives. The case movement scale developed by the Community Service Society is also assessed.

Trice, Andrew M., and Wood, Samuel E. "Measurement of Recreation Benefits." LAND ECONOMICS 34 (August 1958): 195–207.

> The California Department of Water Resources in 1957 developed benefit measures defining the potential recreational use of a series of reservoirs. A system of concentric travel cost zones was designed to serve this purpose.

Tropman, John E., and Gohlke, Karl H. "Cost/Benefit Analysis: Toward Comprehensive Planning in the Criminal Justice System." CRIME AND DELIN-QUENCY 19 (July 1973): 315–22.

> The authors urge practitioners to use the approach to better address the policy concerns of their agencies. They state their view that it facilitates better decision making by developing the information needed for better decisions, by systematizing the process, and by developing the budget calculuses explicit and implicit in decisions.

U.S. Comptroller General. REPORT TO THE CONGRESS OF THE UNITED STATES: AN OVERVIEW OF BENEFIT COST-ANALYSIS FOR WATER RESOURCES PROJECTS--IMPROVEMENTS STILL NEEDED. Washington, D.C.: General Accounting Office, 7 August 1978. Chap. 3: 9 p.

> This report argues that regulations for economic evaluation are inadequate and frequently lack formal criteria to document the validity of some benefits. Regions and districts within the same federal agency use different assumptions to compute the same benefits. Recreation, area redevelopment, and navigation bene-fits are then reviewed in the context of these regulations.

U.S. Congress. Joint Economic Committee. BENEFIT-COST ANALYSIS OF FEDERAL PROGRAMS. 92d Cong., 2d sess. Joint Committee Print. Com-pendium of papers submitted to the Subcommittee on Priorities and Economy in Government. Washington, D.C.: Government Printing Office, January 1973. 52 p.

> This is a collection of federal agency responses to questions about the extent of their use of program evaluation and benefit-cost techniques.

_____. THE PROGRAM FOR BETTER JOBS AND INCOME: AN ANALYSIS
OF COSTS AND DISTRIBUTIONAL EFFECTS. 95th Cong., 2d sess. Joint
Committee Print. Washington, D.C.: Government Printing Office, February
1978. 14 p.

> Robert Haveman and Eugene Smolensky evaluate the Carter ad-
> ministration's welfare proposal by developing a series of new
> alternatives as variations on the original proposal: single tier
> negative income tax, retention, or elimination of the earned
> income tax credit; increasing the incentive to take a regular
> rather than special Title IX job; increasing the Title IX wage
> rate above the minimum wage; making Title IX jobs available
> to all primary earners; and capping the job component with a
> ceiling of 800,000 new jobs. The alternatives are each
> weighed against such criteria as federal cash benefits, the num-
> ber of SSI and AFDC recipients made "worse off," the number
> of job slots, and the costs of the job program and the earned
> income tax credit.

U.S. Congress. Office of Technology Assessment. POLICY IMPLICATIONS
OF THE COMPUTED TOMOGRAPHY (CT) SCANNER. Washington, D.C.:
Congressional Office of Technology Assessment, August 1978. 195 p.

> A major focus of this report is the definition of efficacy per-
> formance criteria. Efficacy of new technology is evaluated in
> terms of the benefits individuals receive and the probability of
> that benefit; the population benefiting; the medical problem af-
> fected; and the conditions of use under which the technology is
> found to be beneficial. Five formulations of efficacy for diagnos-
> tic technologies are detailed: technical capability; diagnostic ac-
> curacy; diagnostic impact; therapeutic impact; and patient outcome.

Vancil, Richard F. BUREAU OF MINES (A). Boston: Intercollegiate Case
Clearing House, 1967. Case 9-112-040: 15 p.; teaching note 5-112-085:
10 p.

> The Civil Service Commission case examines the concept of in-
> creased governmental purchase of helium (to be stored for the
> next century). Both cost-benefit and discounted cash flow tech-
> niques come into play in the analysis.

_____. FEDERAL AVIATION AGENCY (A). Boston: Intercollegiate Case
Clearing House, 1976. Case 9-111-049: 7 p.; teaching notes 5-111-073: 7 p.;
and 5-176-212: 10 p.

> Costs and savings are estimated for the proposed replacement of
> solid state receivers in FAA facilities by tube-type VHF re-
> ceivers. It was drafted for the Civil Service Commission series.

_____. POST OFFICE DEPARTMENT (C): POSTAL HOLIDAY POLICY. Case
9-111-051. Boston: Intercollegiate Case Clearing House, 1967. 12 p.

The Civil Service Commission case comes from that agency's
issue agenda. Staff is asked to consider whether the agency's
policy of keeping local offices open during local holidays should
be retained or modified.

Weicher, John C. URBAN RENEWAL: NATIONAL PROGRAM FOR LOCAL
PROBLEMS. Washington, D.C.: American Enterprise Institute for Public Policy
Research, December 1972. 96 p.

> This study, like the Anderson analysis (see p. 47) finds little
> justification for urban renewal. Projects have generally been
> inefficient and has made poor people worse off and well-to-do
> people better off. Benefits are discussed at moderate length:
> more efficient land use; increased taxes on project land; benefits
> to nearby property; improved social conditions; and the value of
> new construction.

Wilderman, Elizabeth; Coates, Caroline; and Potter, Alan. A BENEFIT-COST
APPROACH TO MENTAL HEALTH PROGRAM ACCOUNTABILITY ACROSS FISCAL
YEARS. Denver: Fort Logan Mental Health Center, n.d. 19 p.

> Output value analysis, a benefit-cost approach, provides both
> a longitudinal accountability and a method for ascertaining
> changes within the program. Program effectiveness was found
> to remain stable across eight admission cohorts despite dramatic
> decreases in research investment. Staff members were found to
> be decreasing their expectation levels over the course of that
> period of time (for example, dropping self-concept and inter-
> action treatment goals in order to concentrate on more immediate
> medical problems and symptoms reduction goals).

Wolfe, Barbara. "A Cost-Effectiveness Analysis of Reductions in School Expenditures: An Application of an Educational Production Function." JOURNAL
OF EDUCATIONAL FINANCE 2 (Spring 1977): 407-18.

> The author analyzes and compares four alternative school ex-
> penditure scenarios: the same level, with the option of reallo-
> cating up to one third of each resource among achievement sub-
> groups; the same level and the option of reallocating up to one
> third of each resource among a combination of school inputs, and
> achievement subgroups, following cost-effectiveness procedures;
> across-the-board budget reductions of $30 per pupil; and cost-
> effectiveness based budget reduction of $30 per pupil. The au-
> thor recommends the cost-effectiveness techniques to improve
> schools' efficiency, claims that pupil achievement growth is not
> directly tied to expenditure per pupil, and argues for systematic
> rather than across-the-board cuts to exploit current resources
> better.

Wolfe, Sidney M., and Bogue, Ted. "CAT Scanners: Is Fancier Technology Worth a Billion Dollars of Health Consumers' Money?" COMPUTED AXIAL TOMOGRAPHY 1 (January 1977): 59-68.

> This is a collection of reports and memoranda drafted by the Public Citizen Health Research Group, based upon drafts of the Congressional Office of Technology Assessment study and other current primary research data. Costs are detailed in terms of purchase, maintenance, and profits (as the excess of charges over operating costs). Medical benefits and cost savings are detailed, radiation risks are noted, and the question of "how many" CAT scanners are needed is raised.

Wortzman, George; Holgate, Richard; and Morgan, Peter. "Cranial Computed Tomography: An Evaluation of Cost Effectiveness." RADIOLOGY 117 (October 1975): 75-77.

> This article is a major source in the early stages of analysis of the utility of a new high-cost medical technological break-through. The effectiveness standards employed included: alternative tests precluded (170 air studies and 171 angiographic procedures for the 444 patients reviewed); hospital admissions found to be unnecessary (for 58 percent of the outpatients examined); and hospital stays shortened for inpatients.

Zeckhauser, Richard, and Nichols, Albert, eds. BENEFIT-COST AND POLICY ANALYSIS 1974. Chicago: Aldine Publishing Co., 1975. 514 p.

> Especially interesting items include Graham Allison's teaching exercise, an implementation problem concerning the development of a Massachusetts State Medical School; ten wise adages on issue or program analysis from Alain Enthoven; Joseph Newhouse, Charles Phelps, and William Schwartz on alternative national health policies; John Rawls on distributional equity; and W. Lee Hansen and Robert J. Lampman on basic opportunity grants. In the introductory article, John Gilbert, Richard Light, and Frederick Mosteller analyse the randomized field trial program evaluation question. Their review of forty major program evaluations, as well as medical examples, indicates that trials are feasible, produce different results, and flush out small positive results worth considering.

POLITICAL AND ORGANIZATIONAL

FEASIBILITY CRITERIA

Adrian, Charles R. "Leadership and Decision-Making in Manager Cities, A Study of Three Communities." PUBLIC ADMINISTRATION REVIEW 18 (Summer 1958): 208-13.

> In three Michigan cities (in the fifty to eighty thousand population range) with council-manager forms of government, city managers and their staff are the principal sources of policy innovation and leadership. City council members provide less leadership than they theoretically are supposed to provide, and city managers often attribute innovations to technical experts or citizens groups. Examining thirty key issues in the three cities during five years, the manager assumed leadership on fifteen; outside groups, ten; the council, seven; and the mayor, two.

Alford, Robert R. BUREAUCRACY AND PARTICIPATION: POLITICAL CULTURES IN FOUR WISCONSIN CITIES. Chicago: Rand McNally and Co., 1969. 244 p.

> In examining Green Bay, Kenosha, Racine, and Madison, the author views the character of the economic base (trading, manufacturing, and professional center) as a crucial independent variable for the study of the political process. The cities are analyzed in terms of the coalitions of their elites, the prevailing ideology or ethos, institutional patterns, and the frequency and intensity of elite and nonelite participation in urban decisions. The author contributes a useful definition of how the resolution of issues helps to lay out policy.

_____. HEALTH CARE POLITICS: IDEOLOGICAL AND INTEREST GROUP BARRIERS TO REFORM. Chicago: University of Chicago Press, 1974. 294 p.

> The author, influenced by Murray Edelman's arguments, proposes that the rational content of ideology is almost irrelevant to the social function of the ideas (for example: reassurance to a group or the presentation of a political challenge to the power of a group). In a study of New York City health reform commissions's analyses, he finds the recommendations to be more often adminis-

trative than substantive. In reviewing the development of
neighborhood family-care centers, he sees three groups com-
peting for policy goals--professional monopolists, corporate ra-
tionalizers, and consumer equal-health advocates. The latter
group, lacking continuing constituencies, falls prey to coopta-
tion by the other interests.

Allen, Ivan, Jr., with Hemphill, Paul. MAYOR: NOTES ON THE SIXTIES.
New York: Simon and Schuster, 1971. 255 p.

This memoir describes the symbolic leadership a mayor can offer
a community on divisive social issues--specifically racial mod-
eration during a period of change in the South. There is also
a good deal of description of both the limitations and the potential of mayoral office, on a day-by-day operational level.

Altshuler, Alan A. THE CITY PLANNING PROCESS: A POLITICAL ANALYSIS.
Ithaca, N.Y.: Cornell University Press, 1964. 466 p.

The author studies the role of planners, potentially an example
of great local governmental discretionary authority, in order to
explore how in fact strategic value choices are determined.
Four case studies in Minneapolis and St. Paul detail the development of two general plans and the locational decisions for
two public projects. The author notes the tendency of the profession to avoid conflict by eschewing all but the most predic-
table effects of actions. Further the political culture of the
Twin Cities tended to inhibit the development of conditions in
which comprehensive planning could have great impact.

Anderson, James E. PUBLIC POLICY-MAKING. New York: Praeger Publishers,
1975. 178 p.

Of particular interest in chapter 3 is the clear, accessible treatment of what is a policy agenda. The author works with the
theories of Roger Cobb and Charles D. Elder on the agenda, and
David Truman on interest groups. Two cases are offered as ex-
amples--coal mine safety and environmental pollution control.

Bachrach, Peter, and Baratz, Morton S. "Decisions and Nondecisions: An
Analytic Framework." AMERICAN POLITICAL SCIENCE REVIEW 57 (September
1963): 632-42.

The authors propose, in this important article, that community
decision-making researchers have ignored "nondecisionmaking,"
the manipulation of dominant community values, myths, and political institutions and procedures to limit the scope of decision
making on safe issues. The authors also distinguish the concepts
of power, authority, influence, manipulation, and force from
one another, as they propose to lay the groundwork for new empirical research.

_____. POWER AND POVERTY: THEORY AND PRACTICE. New York: Oxford University Press, 1970. 220 p.

> The authors' earlier view of the nondecision concept is explored empirically in this review of the antipoverty political process in Baltimore. They state their belief that influential business leaders used the issue of equal opportunity to divert public attention from the question of what actual share militant organizations should have in the making of community decisions. Antipoverty programs, as political catalysts, provide the poor with areas of conflict, sources of power, incentive for conflict, and a doctrine of legitimacy.

Banfield, Edward C. BIG CITY POLITICS. New York: Random House, 1965. 149 p.

> Colleagues like Martha Derthick, James Q. Wilson, and J. David Greenstone contributed to this benchmark inventory of the political process of governing Atlanta, Boston, Detroit, El Paso, Los Angeles, Miami, Philadelphia, St. Louis, and Seattle. The questions raised were the basic ones: how the government is organized; how it really works; how they get elected; interest groups and influentials; how issues are handled.

Banfield, Edward C., and Wilson, James Q. CITY POLITICS. Cambridge: MIT-Harvard Joint Center for Urban Studies, 1963. 362 p.

> This basic text is most memorable for its articulation of such concepts as cleavages and attachments, as well as for its catalog--explanatory introduction to the structure of city politics (distribution of authority, federal relationships, centralization of influence), and political forms and styles (machine, reform, factions, nonpartisanship, the council-manager form, master planning).

Bauer, Raymond A., and Gergen, Kenneth J., eds. THE STUDY OF POLICY FORMATION. New York: Free Press, 1968. 392 p.

> This work is a good summary, as of 1968, of social science's general theoretical development in the area of policy analysis. Among the contributions are Bauer on organizational theory; Richard Zeckhauser and Elmer Schaeffer on the economic theoretical basis for decision analysis; Enid Schoettle on the political science literature; and Gergen on research methods. Especially significant is Gergen's piece called "Assessing the Leverage Points in the Process of Policy Formation," in which he attempts to lay out a model for identifying the key actors on an issue.

Bellush, Jewel, and David, Stephen M. RACE AND POLITICS IN NEW YORK CITY: FIVE STUDIES IN POLICYMAKING. New York: Praeger Publishers, 1971. 202 p.

These cases cover such topics as community mental health care, a police civilian review board, school decentralization, and the scattered-site housing project in Forest Hills. Rich with detail, and thoroughly researched from the files of the relevant public agencies, these cases offer an excellent insight into the operations of the political process in New York during this period.

Berger, Peter L., and Neuhaus, Richard John. TO EMPOWER PEOPLE: THE ROLE OF MEDIATING STRUCTURES IN PUBLIC POLICY. Washington, D.C.: American Enterprise Institute for Public Policy Research, 1977. 45 p. Paperbound.

Four institutions standing between the individual in his private life and the large institutions of public life, are discussed as mediating structures: neighborhood; family; church; and voluntary association. This piece is the philosophic underpinning supporting American Enterprise Institute policy research underway in the areas of health care, housing and zoning, social services and welfare, education, and criminal justice. It argues for a political process which explores how a common purpose may be achieved through the enhancement of myriad particular interests.

Caro, Robert. THE POWER BROKER. New York: Alfred A. Knopf, 1974. 1,279 p.

This biography traces the impact of a single individual upon the social and political processes of New York. The story of Robert Moses's career highlights the relationship between developmental planning and the governmental process, and details the growth of quasi-governmental public authorities under Moses's wing.

Cobb, Roger; Ross, Jennie-Keith; and Ross, Marc Howard. "Agenda Building as a Comparative Political Process." AMERICAN POLITICAL SCIENCE REVIEW 70 (March 1976): 126-38.

The authors propose a model which can account for the variations in the ways in which issues reach the agendas of different city governments. They describe four major characteristics of an issue's career: initiation; specification; expansion; and entrance. Some issues achieve public agenda status, but not formal agenda status. For the authors, reaching only public agenda status may qualify an issue for a nondecision. If a community leaves a large volume of issues in this category, or delays the progress of a great many issues to the formal agenda, these conditions may be indicators of political instability.

Cuban, Larry. URBAN SCHOOL CHIEFS UNDER FIRE. Chicago: University of Chicago Press, 1976. 223 p.

The author, himself a school superintendent, traces the responses of three colleagues in Chicago, Washington, and San Francisco to crises enveloping their offices. The crises include desegregation, independent evaluation, federal funding, and Sputnik. The three political contexts--school organizations, boards of education, and relevant pressure groups--are contrasted. Four leadership concepts are presented: teacher-scholar; negotiator-statesman; corporate administrator; and rational school chief.

Cunningham, James V. URBAN LEADERSHIP IN THE SIXTIES. Cambridge, Mass.: Schenkman Publishing Co., 1970. 93 p.

The author employs Joseph Schumpeter's and Alexander George's definitions of political entrepreneurship to evaluate the work of the mayors of Cleveland, Chicago, New Haven, and Pittsburgh: originality; risk taking; initiative; energy; openness; organizational ability; and promotional ingenuity.

Cuomo, Mario. FOREST HILLS DIARY: THE CRISIS OF LOW-INCOME HOUSING. New York: Random House, 1974. 209 p.

This diary is a fine example of the dispute mediation process surrounding an issue, the introduction of scattered-site public housing into Forest Hills. The author, self-consciously developing an issue analysis, provides some incisive commentary on the nature of public interest analysis.

Dahl, Robert A. WHO GOVERNS? DEMOCRACY AND POWER IN AN AMERICAN CITY. New Haven, Conn.: Yale University Press, 1961. 355 p.

In one of the basic studies of democratic pluralism, the author defines consensus as a recurring process of interchange among political professionals, the political stratum, and the great bulk of the population. The research undertaken in New Haven tracks the interactions of decision makers in regard to political nominations, urban renewal, and education.

Davies, J. Clarence III. NEIGHBORHOOD GROUPS AND URBAN RENEWAL. New York: Columbia University Press, 1966. 235 p.

After reviewing three New York City urban renewal case studies, the author explores group and individual motivations, especially the bases for their level of active participation. Also addressed are neighborhood versus city-wide public interest questions.

Downs, Anthony. INSIDE BUREAUCRACY. Boston: Little, Brown, and Co., 1966. 292 p.

The author develops a series of propositions about bureau behavior, assuming rational goal attainment by bureaucrats, who are nevertheless significantly influenced by their own self-interest and a strong relationship between an organization's social functions and its internal structure. Advocacy and zealotry, and

75

conserving and climbing, are compared as leadership styles.
Life cycle is defined in terms of response to expansion and
shrinkage of functions. Also defined are: relationships to the
environment; communications; control processes and problems;
"the rigidity cycle"; the dynamics of search and change; terri-
toriality; ideologies; and goal consensus, recruitment, and in-
doctrination.

Eyestone, Robert. THE THREADS OF PUBLIC POLICY: A STUDY IN POLICY
LEADERSHIP. Indianapolis: Bobbs-Merrill Co., 1971. 197 p.

The author believes that city governments may fail to meet the
standards which urban critics define as necessary for delivering
city services. He feels that elected city officials may con-
sciously choose not to do so. This work studies how policy
leadership in city councils, which is possible when opportunities
arise, is perceived by politicians, and how it can legally and
politically be handled via preferred alternative courses of action.

Frey, Frederick W. "Comment: On Issues and Nonissues in the Study of Power."
AMERICAN POLITICAL SCIENCE REVIEW 65 (December 1971): 1091-101.

The author discusses research on issue resolution, as validations
of viewpoints in the pluralist-elitist debate. He notes that
while issues may be selected because of their representativeness
or their importance, there is no agreed-upon sampling procedure
for their identification. He discusses nonissues in terms of two
discernible characteristics--expectation and prevention--and
urges their study, particularly because their disposition in such
a fashion may be essential to the system. If so, the process
which provides their elimination should be scrutinized.

Gordon, Diana R. CITY LIMITS: BARRIERS TO CHANGE IN URBAN GOV-
ERNMENT. New York: Charterhouse, 1973. 329 p.

This New York City policy analyst writes about six attempts at
innovative programming during the Lindsay administration, and
about the conflict between the needs for structural and programmatic change. The cases themselves are quite interesting; they
discuss heroin, lead poisoning, welfare hotels, a new city water
tunnel, a community center, and prison reform.

Hargrove, Erwin C. THE MISSING LINK: THE STUDY OF THE IMPLEMENTA-
TION OF SOCIAL POLICY. Paper 797-1. Washington, D.C.: Urban Institute,
July 1975. 128 p. Paperbound.

This paper attempts to identify the kinds of research knowledge
which might help government to design and implement programs
better. Policy analysis, policy research, and social science
research are the three areas of knowledge surveyed. The policy
analyst is viewed as the synthesizer of research who would help

the program manager act more prudently on an operational level.

Henry, Edward L., ed. MICROPOLIS IN TRANSITION: A STUDY OF A SMALL CITY. Collegeville, Minn.: St. John's University, Center for the Study of Local Government, 1971. 395 p.

> The former mayor of St. Cloud, Minnesota, who holds a doctorate in political science, lays out the policymaking environment and a series of case studies on the political process of this small "outstate growth center." The case studies detail such policy problems as the taxing of a big utility, delay in improving an obsolescent physical infrastructure, airport development, air pollution control authority, "crossroads center" annexation, and the problem of "the dam nobody wanted."

Howitt, Arnold. "Big City Mayors: Strategies of Governing." Cambridge, Mass.: Harvard University, Department of City and Regional Planning, August 1977. 18 p. Mimeo.

> The author defines the agenda of a big-city mayor in terms of how and why a mayor allocates his limited resources of time and influence in such areas as oversight of service delivery, innovation, the budget process, and conflict management. He finds local government to have been most influenced during the last decade by expanding scope, increasingly complex intergovernmental relations, expanded nonelectoral political participation, the changing character of public issues and conflict, cycles of fiscal expansion and contraction, and the erosion of stable sources of political power outside government.

_____. ELECTORAL CONSTRAINTS ON MAYORAL BEHAVIOR. Discussion paper D77-4. Cambridge, Mass.: Harvard University Department of City and Regional Planning, April 1977. 41 p. Paperbound.

> The author proposes that the traditional electoral accountability model be varied according to variations in the structure of electoral competition and political communication. In examining the cases of Boston and Philadelphia, the author finds that mayors tend to be responsive in terms of broad outlines of activity, rather than specific actions. Mayors of large cities cannot adequately receive and respond to unaggregated demands made by the small political organizations that flourish in most cities.

_____. MAYORS AND POLICY INNOVATION. Discussion paper D77-13. Cambridge, Mass.: Harvard University Department of City and Regional Planning, September 1977. 23 p. Paperbound.

> Mayors might choose to promote innovation within their administrations for electoral reasons (to enfranchise uninvolved groups; because of ambition for higher office; in terms of visibility to their constituency; or perhaps in response to campaign pledges),

due to bureaucratic demands, or as a result of changes in the external environment (federal or state efforts; constituency attitudes; financial inducements; single events). This piece also details the potential impact of timing criteria upon mayoral decisions.

Huitt, Ralph. "Political Feasibility." In POLITICAL SCIENCE AND PUBLIC POLICY, edited by Austin Ranney, pp. 263-75. Chicago: Markham, 1968.

This essay lays out familiar democratic pluralist arguments about the incrementalism of the American political system, but the discussion of how to gain presidential and congressional assent for decisions begins to describe some dimensions of the feasibility question.

Hunter, Floyd. COMMUNITY POWER STRUCTURE: A STUDY OF DECISION MAKERS. Garden City, N.Y.: Anchor Books, 1963. 294 p.

Originally published in 1953, this is the most influential of the studies of the local power elite, "the power structure." Atlanta, in the author's view, is run by a small group of powerful men who are held together by social and business connections. The economic interests are said to dominate the policymaking process. These findings are based upon a reputational rankings system designed to define who the city's top leaders are, and upon the tracing of their interactions on such issues as bringing a new industry to the city; testimony before Congress on a tax bill; and review of an annexation development plan before the city.

Hyman, Herbert Harvey, ed. THE POLITICS OF HEALTH CARE: NINE CASE STUDIES OF INNOVATIVE PLANNING IN NEW YORK CITY. New York: Praeger Publishers, 1973. 208 p.

Using a modification of Roland Warren's action-system model, nine cases in health policy in New York City are presented in such areas as: family planning; Medicaid; ghetto medicine; the public hospital system's comprehensive planning; rat control; abortion; ambulatory care; and regional medical programs. The case writers each detail who the decision makers were in determining the nature of the issue; what their objectives were, and for whom they were targeted; and what happened to these objectives after opposition developed.

Judd, Dennis R., and Mendelson, Robert E. THE POLITICS OF URBAN PLANNING: THE EAST ST. LOUIS EXPERIENCE. Urbana: University of Illinois Press, 1973. 241 p.

This series of East St. Louis case studies interprets failures in the redevelopment process in terms of stresses between the professional planners and the political forces in the community. In particular, there is discussion of the preoccupation of planners with the design of, rather than the implementation of, plans.

Kaplan, Harold. URBAN RENEWAL POLITICS: SLUM CLEARANCE IN NEWARK. New York: Columbia University Press, 1963. 219 p.

> Newark's housing authority launched nine slum clearance and urban-renewal projects between 1949 and 1960. The author details the roles of the groups whose political support was needed to implement these projects--nonlocal participants, politicos, realtors, corporation executives, city planners, and grass roots organizations.

Keyes, Langley. THE REHABILITATION PLANNING GAME: A STUDY IN THE DIVERSITY OF NEIGHBORHOOD. Cambridge: MIT Press, 1969. 253 p.

> These Boston case studies provide good tangible examples of the frequent need to respond to neighborhood satisfaction criteria, when either developing a plan or framing a decision. A good institutional biography of a redevelopment agency is also included.

Kotter, John P., and Lawrence, Paul. MAYORS IN ACTION: FIVE APPROACHES TO URBAN GOVERNANCE. New York: John Wiley and Sons, 1974. 278 p.

> In a study of twenty mayors, five mayoral behavior patterns are detailed--ceremonial, caretaker, personality-individualist, executive, and program entrepreneur. The quality of the impact of these different types of mayoralty is dependent upon the success of the mayors in coaligning themselves properly with their cities, networks, and agendas. There is an interesting and anecdote-laden discussion of mayoral agenda-setting, ranging from the approach of the rational-deductive planner to the approach of the "muddler."

Lindsay, John V. THE CITY. New York: W.W. Norton and Co., 1969. 224 p.

> This book is interesting in its descriptions of how an activist social progressive perceives his role as major. The discussions of meetings with staff on budget plans and the delivery of public services, for example, indicate how a proactive view of mayoral leadership can be operationalized.

Long, Norton E. "The Local Community as an Ecology of Games." AMERICAN JOURNAL OF SOCIOLOGY 64 (November 1958): 251-61.

> The author argues that a great deal of community activities consist of the undirected cooperation of particular social structures, each seeking particular goals and, in doing so, meshing with others. Within structured community games, behavior is characterized by goals, norms, strategies, and roles.

Lynn, Laurence E., Jr. "Implementation: Will the Hedgehogs Be Outfoxed?" POLICY ANALYSIS 3 (Spring 1977): 277-80.

The writer responds to the emergence of policy implementation research by asking some basic questions: How frequently are ideas which fail in implementation "bad ideas" or unacceptable ideas? Is there a stock of good ideas waiting to be implemented? Does failure in implementation sometimes result from failing to respect decentralized and pluralistic processes?

Martin, Roscoe C.; Munger, Frank; et al. DECISIONS IN SYRACUSE: A METROPOLITAN ACTION STUDY. Bloomington: University of Indiana Press, 1961. 368 p.

These case studies suggest, according to the author, that Syracuse has no single center of power; that decision-making power is fragmented around the institutions, agencies, and individuals associated most closely with specific issues; and that many different kinds of community power can be defined.

Meltsner, Arnold J. "Political Feasibility and Policy Analysis." PUBLIC ADMINISTRATION REVIEW 32 (November-December 1972): 859-67.

The author sketches the bridge from decision analysis to issue analysis, the addition of political and organizational feasibility criteria, to the set of cost and performance criteria for decision making. He lays out categories for review such as the identification of actors, their beliefs, motivations, and resources, and the sites of their interactions.

Merelman, Richard M. "On the Neo-Elitist Critique of Community Power." AMERICAN POLITICAL SCIENCE REVIEW 62 (June 1968): 451-60.

The author writes that neoelitist criticism of pluralism is based on their beliefs that elites can create false consensuses and manipulate the values of nonelites; elites can limit the scope of initiation of conflict over issues; and coercive actions and sanctions may stop government from ever acting on issues. The article challenges these premises and proposes that no elite can operate for long solely on the basis of not making decisions.

Merton, Robert K. "Types of Influentials: The Local and the Cosmopolitan." In COMMUNICATIONS RESEARCH 1948-1949, edited by Paul F. Lazarsfeld and Frank N. Stanton, pp. 189-202. New York: Harper and Brothers, 1949.

Community influentials can be described as either local or cosmopolitan in orientation. These groups differ in their commitment to remain in the community, their inclination to establish frequent contacts with a great many neighbors, and their preferences in voluntary organizations. The cosmopolitan is sought out for his or her specialized skills or experience, while the local is sought out for his or her intimate appreciation of intangible but affectively significant details.

Meyerson, Martin, and Banfield, Edward C. POLITICS, PLANNING, AND THE PUBLIC INTEREST: THE CASE OF PUBLIC HOUSING IN CHICAGO. New York: Free Press, 1965. 353 p.

> This classic case study is invaluable both in its depiction of the policymaking process and environment surrounding public housing issues, and in its conceptualization of "planning" and "the public interest," using the case study to illuminate the application of these concepts. Banfield, for example, clearly draws out the rational decision analysis model, as he discusses norms such as "comprehensivism," and city-wide versus neighborhood interest conflicts.

Mowitz, Robert J., and Wright, Deil S. PROFILE OF A METROPOLIS: A CASE BOOK. Detroit: Wayne State University Press, 1962. 678 p.

> Ten case studies examine crucial decisions and events in the Detroit metropolitan area between 1945 and 1960. The cases focus on, for example, inner city redevelopment, urban renewal, water resources, airport site selection, an expressway extension, the St. Lawrence Seaway, relief drains, and annexation. Overall, the authors anticipate no particular growth of metropolitan institutions to replace the "pluralistic" current governance system.

Niskanen, William A., Jr. BUREAUCRACY AND REPRESENTATIVE GOVERN-MENT. Chicago: Aldine Publishing Co., 1971. 241 p.

> This work reflects the systems analysts's view that bureaucrats do not invariably act in the public interest. The author's theory is that bureau administrators operate from a "supply" view of the public services that might be provided to their environment. Also defined is an aggregate theory of the behavior of representative government in formulating demand. Recommendations for changes in the bureaucracy, the sources of supply of public services, and American political institutions generally are presented with the hope of improving the performance of the public service delivery system.

Petshek, Kirk R. THE CHALLENGE OF URBAN REFORM: POLICIES AND PROGRAMS IN PHILADELPHIA. Philadelphia: Temple University Press, 1973. 336 p.

> The author, Philadelphia's city economist, writes about the policies and programs for the reform mayoralties of Joseph Clark and Richardson Dilworth. These administrations came to view the city in terms of impulses toward comprehensive program coordination, a need for economic indicators and measurements to trace whether revenues will support long-term goals, the potential for nonprofit corporation action on city problems, and the definition of new priorities, which themselves are practical political and social goals.

Polsby, Nelson W. COMMUNITY POWER AND POLITICAL THEORY. New Haven, Conn.: Yale University Press, 1963. 144 p.

> The author works with Robert Dahl and Raymond Wolfinger's New Haven research, and positions their findings on power, community structure, and the political process in response to the earlier contributions of the community studies. He lays out the pluralist alternative approach to the study of community power, urging researchers to study issue-areas which are important to the life of the community, the actual behavior of participants, as well as their reputations, and the outcomes of actual decisions, as well as motivations.

Powledge, Fred. MODEL CITY. New York: Simon and Schuster, 1970. 350 p.

> This is a vivid muckraking journalistic account of the New Haven redevelopment program, providing a great deal of descriptive detail on the urban political process.

Pressman, Jeffrey L. FEDERAL PROGRAMS AND CITY POLITICS: THE DYNAMICS OF THE AID PROCESS IN OAKLAND. Berkeley: University of California Press, 1975. 162 p.

> The author describes how a retrenchment-oriented city government can blunt federal intervention efforts in Oakland. He details the development of a new political arena, the antipoverty programs, and the impact upon that arena of the city-wide government process. In analyzing "donor-recipient" relationships, he argues for more performance-based and implementation-oriented federal approaches in preference to federal requirements for comprehensive planning.

_____. PRECONDITIONS OF MAYORAL LEADERSHIP. Working paper no. 129. Berkeley: University of California, Institute of Urban and Regional Development, August 1970. 91 p. Paperbound.

> This report details how well Oakland's mayoralty performed against a series of standards for mayoral leadership: sufficient financial and staff resources (almost nonexistent); city control over social problems areas (outside city hall's control); a full-time executive (a $7,500 per year salary); mayoral staff for policy planning (one assistant); media vehicles for publicity (good rapport with the only major paper); and politically oriented leadership which can be mobilized to support particular goals (absent).

Pressman, Jeffrey L., and Wildavsky, Aaron. IMPLEMENTATION. Berkeley and Los Angeles: University of California Press, 1973. 182 p.

> This is a study of the ordinary circumstances which forestall implementation of a decision. Part of the Oakland Project series, it has sparked the implementation literature on the organizational

feasibility of carrying out public objectives. Oakland's economic development program fails as basic agreements slowly dissolve, in part because of the widely differing perspectives of a multitude of participants.

Rabinovitz, Francine F. CITY POLITICS AND PLANNING. New York: Atherton Press, 1969. 192 p.

In a comparative analysis of the role of the physical planner in six cities, the author examines the political roles which a planner may assume (technician, broker, and mobilizer) in different types of communities (cohesive, executive-centered, competitive, and fragmented). Resources of the planner (expertise, information and invention, bureaucratic position, time, and motivation, and access to other resources) are compared with the constraints operating against a planner's success (planning norms, the planner's own needs, and the impact of these two considerations).

Rogers, David. THE MANAGEMENT OF BIG CITIES: INTEREST GROUPS AND SOCIAL CHANGE STRATEGIES. Beverly Hills, Calif.: Sage Publications, 1971. 189 p.

This book was developed from federally funded research on how interorganizational relationships in inner cities affect the implementation of social development programs. The author sketches the power structures in New York, Philadelphia, and Cleveland, by examining the extent to which power is concentrated or dispersed, the organization and functioning of city government, the relationships between major interest groups and coalitions within cities, and city relationships with federal and state agencies. Implementation, the author believes, is hindered by fragmentation and baronial power seeking.

_____. 110 LIVINGSTON STREET: POLITICS AND BUREAUCRACY IN THE NEW YORK CITY SCHOOLS. New York: Random House, 1968. 584 p.

This author presents a memorable case study in urban service bureaucracy during the period from 1963 to 1968. He describes the board of education's organizational defenses that allow it to function in what he calls unprofessional, undemocratic, and politically costly ways.

Rosen, Harry, and Metsch, Jonathan M. "Problems in PSRO Implementation." JOURNAL OF HEALTH POLITICS, POLICY, AND LAW 1 (Winter 1977): 391-97.

The writers employ innovation theory to illuminate the implementation problems confronting PSROs (Professional Standards Review Organizations). For example, they propose that potential sponsoring organizations be evaluated in terms of their innovative potential, as well as in terms of political feasibility (particularly medical societies). The extensive use of nonphysicians in the review process is viewed as a risk-aversion tactic by the physician community.

Selznick, Philip. LEADERSHIP IN ADMINISTRATION. New York: Harper and Row, 1957. 162 p.

Highly normative in its approach to organizational leadership, this familiar volume defines and addresses the concept of institutionalization. To curb organizational rivalry and other negative consequences, the author argues that a leader must work to commit the organization's personnel to an institutional embodiment of purpose. Spontaneous social and informal forces should be mobilized behind this commitment, not allowed to form an opposition to its implementation.

Sofen, Edward. THE MIAMI METROPOLITAN EXPERIMENT: A METROPOLITAN ACTION STUDY. Rev. ed. Garden City, N.Y.: Anchor Books, 1966. 375 p.

In this volume of the metropolitan action study series which initially presented the Syracuse case study, Dade County's experience is detailed in terms of the absence of countervailing interest groups in the coalition opposing metropolitization, and also in terms of the absence of any semblance of a crisis. One particular area of political conflict within the metropolitan system predictably surrounds the increasing demands of well urbanized but unincorporated areas.

Starr, Roger. "Power and Powerlessness in a Regional City." PUBLIC INTEREST 28 (Summer 1968): 3-24.

Many of the roles played by the mayor of New York City are explored in his article: mythmaker purveying images of this city concerning wealth, glamour, and political liberalism; lobbyist, before Congress, the state legislature, the city council, and the Board of Estimate; and chief employer.

Talbot, Allan R. THE MAYOR'S GAME: RICHARD LEE OF NEW HAVEN AND THE POLITICS OF CHANGE. New York: Praeger Publishers, 1967. 274 p.

This description of Richard Lee's administration in New Haven demonstrates the capacity for social intervention of an activist mayor committed to providing moral public leadership. This book is really a biography of that mayoralty, detailing each of the social and physical redevelopment efforts, and their political implementation.

Wildavsky, Aaron. "The Analysis of Issue-Contexts in the Study of Decision-Making." JOURNAL OF POLITICS 24 (November 1962): 717-32.

This article proposes that the study of issue decisions take into
account underlying and related issues, and the nature of the
policymaking environment. For example, the Dixon-Yates controversy should be understood within the context of private
versus public power arguments.

_____. LEADERSHIP IN A SMALL TOWN. Totowa, N.J.: Bedminister Press,
1964. 388 p.

In this pluralist study of who governs in Oberlin, the author
first examines the level of interest and activity in public affairs,
and its distribution within the community, and then provides
case history vignettes about Oberlin's leadership. Leaders and
nonleaders are then surveyed, and their responses compared to
the findings derived from the case studies.

Williams, Walter, ed. "Special Issue on Implementation." POLICY ANALYSIS
1 (Summer 1975): 451-566.

This collection of articles details how to move from making a
decision, to operationalizing that decision. Richard F. Elmore
traces how experimental design in the follow-through educational
program bowed to political considerations. David P. Weikart
and Bernard A. Banet describe how difficult it was to encourage
teachers to experiment with their learning concepts in their own
classrooms. Edward M. Gramlich and Patricia P. Koshel discuss
the impact of acting in extreme haste upon OEO's educational performance contracting experiment. Williams lays out
a model for implementation analysis: technical capacity; political feasibility; and the technical and political strategies for
implementation.

Wilson, James Q. "The Mayors vs. the Cities." PUBLIC INTEREST 28
(Summer 1968): 25-37.

The writer, worried that large city mayors continue to manifest
liberal tendencies amid increasingly conservative constituencies,
proposes an explanation. Mayors are responding not to their
constituencies, but to their "audiences," made up of federal
officials, foundation executives, the news media, and suburban
residents who might choose to vote for their election to statewide offices. These audiences may control such resources as
funds which could be made available for innovative programs to
be funded outside city budget constraints, and the availability
of potentially talented staff people interested in joining a city
administration.

Wolfinger, Raymond E. "Nondecisions and the Study of Local Politics."
AMERICAN POLITICAL SCIENCE REVIEW 65 (December 1971): 1063-80.

This essay is a response to Bachrach's and Baratz's nondecisions arguments (see p. 72). There is discussion of the criteria to be employed in selecting the issues to be studied in the community power studies. The writer disputes the Bachrach and Baratz suspicions about the role of businessmen regarding urban renewal in New Haven, stating that the mayor controlled their participation. He wonders whether nondecisions can be distinguished from those issue areas to which leaders assign low priorities, and urges clearer definition of potential candidates for nondecision status.

_____. THE POLITICS OF PROGRESS. Englewood Cliffs, N.J.: Prentice-Hall, 1974. 416 p.

In this analysis of New Haven's political process, the author describes how innovative policies are conceived and executed, in part by exploring the environment surrounding, and the techniques and limitations upon political leadership. He writes, for example, that mayoral careers are strongly affected by the impact of city government on everyday life, the accountability of the mayor for the performance of the city, and easy accessibility.

OBJECTIVES SETTING

"Accountability Symposium." AMERICAN VOCATIONAL JOURNAL 48 (March 1973): 24-60.

> Carl Schaefer, in a lead article, points out that goal achievement should be easily validated in vocational programs, strengthening their position within educational systems. Jess Banks discusses the application of MBO techniques in the overall manpower training field. Gene M. Love argues that the approach can properly be employed to focus on individual performance and needs. John E. Elias and Barry L. Reece propose that vocational educators examine both competencies and job placement outcomes. Nellie R. McCool discusses accountability for counselors.

Ahart, Gregory J. "Evaluating Contract Compliance: Federal Contracts in Nonconstruction Industries." CIVIL RIGHTS DIGEST 7 (Fall 1974): 34-45.

> The affirmative action plan goals and timetables of nonconstruction businesses are to be reviewed by the contract compliance offices of appropriate federal agencies. This article describes the character of the federal regulatory effort, identifying the weakness of the performance review aspect of this system of management objectives.

Ahlberg, Nancy, and Christenson, Charles. PROGRAM EVALUATION IN EAST WINDSOR REGIONAL SCHOOL DISTRICT (A) AND (B). Cases C16-76-088-9. Cambridge, Mass.: Kennedy School of Government, 1976. Case (A): 15 p.; case (B): 15 p.

> The cases detail the difficulties of developing a curriculum by the objectives accountability model. Criterion-referenced tests of social science objectives must be designed with the help of both school system teacher panels and outside consultants. The pressure from the public for standardized tests compromises these efforts. The cases offer extraordinary insight into the subject of accountability, and its relationship to MBO questions generally.

Aplin, John C., Jr., and Schoderbek, Peter P. "How to Measure MBO."
PUBLIC PERSONNEL MANAGEMENT 5 (March–April 1976): 88–95.

> This very sound piece derives interesting methodology for pro-
> gram design from MBO logic, although needs analysis questions
> are not addressed. The authors also properly focus attention on
> the relationship between program objectives and strategic plan-
> ning goals. In a survey of social service administrators, they
> found that of the 82 percent of the respondents using MBO,
> 86.5 percent felt that their future evaluations and rewards would
> be based upon their performance under MBO.

Association of the Bar of the City of New York. Committee on Civil
Rights. THE USE OF QUOTAS, GOALS, AND AFFIRMATIVE ACTION PRO-
GRAMS TO OVERCOME THE EFFECTS OF RACIAL DISCRIMINATION. New
York: n.d. 22 p.

> The committee argues that quotas and goals should be used with
> great care as an interim step, because a reexamination of so-
> ciety's decision-making criteria is called for and is long overdue.
> Quotas might be employed, for example, to correct the effects
> of past discrimination, serving as an ameliorative step, rather
> than as a guarantee of a permanent vested right. Footnotes
> provide examples of goals language to be found in affirmative
> action plans.

Audette, Donna M. "Activities of the Follow-Up Unit." In PROGRAM EVALUA-
TION PROJECT REPORT, 1969-1973, chapter 2. Minneapolis, Minn.: Program
Evaluation Resource Center, June 1974.

> This paper traces goal attainment follow-up guide assessment of
> clients' levels of attainment, as well as consumer satisfaction.
> Follow-up guide materials, as well as survey instruments, are
> included in the appendixes.

Austin, Gilbert R. "Evaluation in the '60's--Accountability in the '70's."
PLANNING AND CHANGING 3 (July 1972): 8-17.

> The writer proposes operationalizing the accountability approach
> by turning elementary school principals into master teachers, by
> asking principals and teachers to design more limited and prac-
> tically attainable goals, by challenging the claims of textbook
> and curricular materials companies, and by promoting team
> learning.

Babcock, Richard, and Sorensen, Peter F., Jr. "A Long-Range Approach to
MBO." MANAGEMENT REVIEW 65 (June 1976): 24-32.

> The authors argue for gradual, phased implementation of the
> approach, consistent with strategic organizational directions.
> MBO often suffers from poor-quality institutionalization. Its

disruptive aspects are too frequently understated, and it should be introduced in a manner designed to provide psychic benefits for personnel.

Badaway, Mahmoud K. "Applying MBO to the Public Sector." BUREAUCRAT 6 (Fall 1977): 3-18.

The writer poses the problem of introducing the approach within service rather than production-oriented organizations. He, however, cites his own experience with a manpower agency, as well as the HEW case, as demonstrations of its benefits. He feels that MBO must be initiated as a self-control rather than as an "imposed control" process. A contingency approach should be developed, and a supportive behavioral climate created and re-enforced.

Barron, Nancy, and Bode, Edward L. "Goal Attainment Scaling and Regionalized Alcohol Program Development." GOAL ATTAINMENT REVIEW 1 (1974): 80-85.

Twelve regional specialists were evaluated according to this sort of procedure, organized around resource development, coordination, and administration goals (really a more traditional MBO review). Six specialists scored poorly, and recommendations are presented to respond to these findings.

Barron, Stephen M. AN APPROACH TO DEVELOPING ACCOUNTABILITY MEASURES FOR THE PUBLIC SCHOOLS. Report P-4464. Santa Monica, Calif.: Rand Corp., September 1970. 30 p.

The author believes that accountability systems depend upon improved, more comprehensive pupil performance measurements, and the ability to estimate the contribution to improved pupil performance by individual teachers, administrators, schools, and districts. Educational systems should be accountable for selecting correct objectives and assigning them appropriate priorities, achieving all of the stated (or implicit objectives), and avoiding unintentional adverse effects upon pupils. Each participant should be held accountable only for those educational outcomes which he or she can affect by actions and decisions. Accountability measures might be used in identifying effective schools, personnel assignment selection, personnel incentives and compensation, improved resource allocation, and program evaluation and research.

Basey, Don M. "MBO in the Department of Education and Science." MANAGEMENT SERVICES IN GOVERNMENT 30 (August 1975): 130-38.

The experience of the British Department of Education and Science was that the approach foundered when applied in an annual review process. The decision was made to narrow the objectives to be reviewed in a more relevant manner, and to conduct reviews at monthly top team meetings. Reviews would focus on what good managers do anyway, based upon instinct and experience. The author's view, however, is that these meetings have been strengthened by the introduction of the process.

Baxter, James W., and Beaulieu, Dean E. "Evaluation of the Adult Outpatient Program, Hennepin County Mental Health Service." In PROGRAM EVALUATION PROJECT REPORT, 1969-1973, chapter 9. Minneapolis, Minn.: Program Evaluation Resource Center, June 1974.

This evaluation indicates that the program has found that goal attainment scaling facilitates analysis of programmatic performance. An adaptation of the procedure allows the manager to generate an index score for various combinations established for the program. Of course, the program also continues to assess individual client progress by applying the technique.

Baydin, Lynda Diane, and Sheldon, Alan P. UNIVERSITY OF MISSOURI-- KANSAS CITY MEDICAL SCHOOL (A) AND (B). Cases 9-474-0767. Boston: Intercollegiate Case Clearing House, 1973. Case (A): 33 p.; case (B): 32 p.

The (B) case outlines the context surrounding institutionalization of the Weed system, the problem-oriented medical record. This approach, employing a numbered problem list as a combined table of contents and index, can be used to identify appropriate goals and objectives for treatment. The (A) case discusses how the goal of developing an educational program to train the general practice "safe physician" was fostered at the University of Missouri.

Beck, Steven; Gale, Melvin; Springer, Kayla; and Spitz, Louis. "An Evaluative Study of Cincinnati General Hospital Psychiatric Emergency Service." GOAL ATTAINMENT REVIEW 2 (1975): 97-108.

The authors propose that they may have found there to be no difference in long-term goal attainment outcome scores among different treatment and discipline variables within their operation. They wonder whether their approach (scales involving treatment motivation, somatic complaints, depression, and employment) may not lend itself to detecting significant differences on such broad independent variables as those analyzed.

Bell, Geneva; Brunson, John; Clark, Toni; Nelson, Roxie; and Stark, Bill. MANUAL OF A SYSTEM OF TREATMENT ACCOUNTABILITY. Snoqualmie, Wash.: Echo Glen Children's Center, Winter 1975. 61 p.

The center has drafted a clearly written manual which outlines staff procedures to be followed in planning and monitoring treatment programs, employing goal attainment scaling methods. Included are worksheets and other skills-training session materials, report forms, and sample individual files. The manual provides a fine introduction to the approach.

Benedict, William. "Utilizing Goal Attainment Scaling to Evaluate a Staff Development Program." GOAL ATTAINMENT REVIEW 1 (1974): 69-79.

A training session for child care workers is described as a model for the use of goal attainment scaling in evaluating staff training projects. The use of the technique within the training process effectively demonstrated how the approach might be employed in daily operational practice.

Berger, Gary S.; Gillings, Dennis B.; and Siegel, Earl. "The Evaluation of Regionalized Perinatal Health Care Programs." AMERICAN JOURNAL OF OBSTETRICS AND GYNECOLOGY 125 (1 August 1976): 924-32.

The evaluation measures progress toward long-term outcome goals (e.g., for five years), by examining how successful different levels of activity are in reaching targets by specific dates (objectives). Weights are allocated to objectives to indicate their relative priority in relationship to goals.

Bitter, James A., and Goodyear, Don L. REHABILITATION EVALUATION: SOME APPLICATION GUIDELINES. New York: MSS Information Corp., 1974. 163 p.

Example 6 of part 2 provides a walk-through approach to the technical aspects of goal attainment scaling. Example 7 introduces Kenneth Reagles's human service scale procedures.

Bledsoe, Ralph C. "Is MBO Working in the Public Sector." Alexandria, Va.: The Bureaucrat Occasional Papers Service, 1975. 17 p.

Given the nature of both the civil service and the political environment, federal MBO holds units, rather than individuals, accountable. The author describes Nixon administration implementation of the approach as characterized by the Office of Management and Budget rather than presidential leadership, bottom-up agency objectives-setting, and problem solving instead of reward and punishment. He argues that communication of intended results internally within public organizations may lead to less defensive behavior, less foot-dragging, and less non-responsiveness.

_____. "MBO and Federal Management: A Retrospective." BUREAUCRAT 2 (Winter 1974): 395-410.

The article places federal MBO efforts within a historical framework of management development activities. For example, there is an identification of the relationship of MBO to the State Department's Policy Analysis and Resource Allocation System and the FAA's Goals Oriented Approach to Planning and Operations.

Bolin, David C., and Kivens, Lawrence. "Evaluation in a Community Mental Health Center: Hennepin County Mental Health Service." EVALUATION 2 (1975): 60-63.

> The article details the history of goal attainment scaling at its point of origination. The agency currently not only still employs the approach in administrative and client-specific goal-setting and follow-up, but also draws upon it for comprehensive evaluation of its service delivery system. A management information system tracks clients from intake through termination for every encounter with the system, and aggregates this data for planning purposes.

Bone, Larry Earl. "The Public Library Goals and Objectives Movement: Death Gasp or Renaissance?" LIBRARY JOURNAL 100 (July 1975): 1283-86.

> Libraries moved into this area in order to clarify their service philosophies, rather than drift with the "accidental pressures of demands." Decentralized approaches have been employed at New York City's branch libraries and through workshops in Tulsa. The author feels that a successful program involves the library staff as a whole. The selection of priorities, such as continuing education and information and referral services, has led to internal political turmoil in Denver and Detroit. However, the author feels that the traditional eclecticism of libraries is ill-suited to the current political climate.

Brady, Rodney H. "MBO Goes to Work in the Public Sector." HARVARD BUSINESS REVIEW 51 (March-April 1973): 65-74.

> In this famous piece on MBO at HEW, there is a presentation of an implementation process, which, as it is described, is quite sensitive to the constraints of public organizations. A very sophisticated definition of a department-wide executive role is included. There are pointed discussions of the need for the development of "stretch" goals, and of the complementary usefulness of issue-oriented conferences during the MBO process.

Brintnall, Joan, and Garwick, Geoffrey, eds. APPLICATIONS OF GOAL ATTAINMENT SCALING. Minneapolis, Minn.: Program Evaluation Resource Center, August 1976. 109 p.

> This is an anthology of short articles and materials drafted by twenty-one different practitioners and academics. An initial presentation by Garwick applies the eight factors of Davis's A-VICTORY model to program evaluation requirements generally and goal attainment scaling specifically. The book also includes collections of readings on outcome feedback and clinicians' reactions, follow-up issues and client-constructed follow-up guides, staff evaluation, reliability and validity, and content analysis.

Brown, David S. "Management by Objectives: Promise and Problems." BU-REAUCRAT 2 (Winter 1974): 411-20.

> Problems in federal government implementation of MBO are detailed: executive-level commitment, participation, and applications in regard to functions not of a control or service nature. The writer proposes a System of Limited Objectives (SLO) focusing on priorities.

Byassee, James, and Tamberino, Edward. "Individually Tailored Behavioral Goals and Therapeutic Summer Camping: A Preliminary Evaluation." GOAL ATTAINMENT REVIEW 2 (1975): 71-78.

> Race and sex differences were found to be significant in the goal attainment evaluation of a small camp program in which children received points that they could cash in for canteen privileges as a reward for goal-oriented behavior.

California. State Department of Health. PATIENT AND PROGRAM EVALUATION RECORDING GUIDE. Sacramento, Calif.: Department of Health, Center for Health Statistics, April 1972. 64 p.

> The guide includes a Weed system-style compendium called the Patient Problem Scale. For each problem, "anchor points" are detailed so that they might be matched to a Staff Effort Scale, establishing appropriate treatment objectives to be attained. Data collected from these procedures can be used for agency resource allocation and planning efforts.

Calsyn, Robert J.; Tornatzky, Louis G.; and Dittmar, Susan. "Incomplete Adoption of an Innovation: The Case of Goal Attainment Scaling." EVALUATION 4 (1977): 127-30.

> The authors find that only 11.3 percent of the agencies employing the approach follow the evaluative research guidelines proposed by Kiresuk and Sherman, who first developed the concept (see p. 113): the setting of treatment goals outside the therapeutic process; unbiased assignment of clients to treatment; and determination of attainment at follow-up by someone other than the therapist.

Campbell, Vincent N., and Nichols, Daryl G. "Setting Priorities Among Objectives." POLICY ANALYSIS 3 (Fall 1977): 561-78.

> The authors favor specifying objectives and their priority before analyzing alternative courses of action, because they fear that difficulties in implementation will forestall efforts to accomplish worthy purposes. They propose the use of benefit ratios to determine priority. Priority is the product of an objective's value when fully achieved, times the discrepancy between current and desired levels of achievement. The value is determined by its

contribution to a comprehensive set of goals of the policymaking body.

Carlson, Georgina D. "Communication Skills Training in a Family Practice Residency Program." GOAL ATTAINMENT REVIEW 1 (1974): 55-68.

Goal attainment scaling was used in conjunction with consumer satisfaction surveys to ascertain whether the program usefully served twelve Hennepin County General Hospital resident physicians. The residents felt that they were "better" able to communicate with their patients.

Carnegie Council on Policy Studies in Higher Education. MAKING AFFIRMATIVE ACTION WORK IN HIGHER EDUCATION. San Francisco: Jossey-Bass Publishers, 1975. 272 p.

Despite difficulties in interpretation of seemingly inconsistent federal policies, the Carnegie Council supports the retention of goals and timetables, because their abandonment, as a federal requirement, could seriously weaken efforts on some campuses, by largely removing the impetus for change. Staffing problems of specific departments, and definitional difficulties about personnel availability are discussed. The University of California at Berkeley's affirmative action plan is evaluated in detail. The Carnegie Council also responds to the most consequential aspect of the MBO performance approach embodied in goals and timetables, by proposing increased efforts on the supply side to recruit women and minority candidates for doctoral study. See particularly chapter 5, "Goals and Timetables."

Carroll, Stephen J., Jr., and Tosi, Henry L. MANAGEMENT BY OBJECTIVES: APPLICATION AND RESEARCH. New York: MacMillan, 1973. 216 p.

The authors argue for formalized institutionalization, since, if formal requirements are not imposed upon managers, they will continue to operate in a style and fashion they believe to be appropriate. Participation by top management is fundamental to effective implementation, and only when each level of management reinforces its use for lower levels by using it itself, are there any real benefits. See particularly chapter 3, "Implementation of MBO."

_____. "The Relationship of Characteristics of the Review Process to the Success of the 'Management by Objectives' Approach." JOURNAL OF BUSINESS 33 (July 1971): 299-305.

The authors find that more frequent performance review leads to more favorable attitudes toward MBO higher goal success, improvements in relationships with the boss, clarity of goals, a feeling that the superior is helpful and supportive, a feeling that the subordinate has influence in matters affecting him, and esteem and satisfaction for the superior.

Christensen, Tom H. MANAGEMENT BY OBJECTIVES AS DECISION MAKING. St. Louis, Mo.: St. Louis University, Center for Urban Programs, Community Residential Treatment Center Institute, December 1975. 28 p.

> This halfway house administrator proposes MBO as the appropriate agency management program, useful for planning, organizing, staffing, directing, and controlling functions. He suggests that performance data helps voluntary agencies to be accountable and assure their organizational survivals.

Churchill, Neil C., and Shank, John K. "Affirmative Action and Guilt-Edged Goals." HARVARD BUSINESS REVIEW 54 (March-April 1976): 111-16.

> The authors propose the use of flow models showing the movement of women and minority group men through each level of management. Reporting requirements are fulfilled in the form of balance sheet and stock summaries of employment data. Also significant would be projections of the rate of flow into different levels of management across a multiyear period. The authors contend that affirmative action goals would be more realistic, if they were based upon rates.

Ciarlo, James. SOME CONSIDERATIONS IN SETTING GOALS FOR COMMUNITY MENTAL HEALTH CENTER PROGRAMS. Denver: Fort Logan Mental Health Center, n.d. 8 p.

> This paper discusses the decision of a center to jettison the single goal of reducing the incidence and prevalence of mental illness in its catchment area. In its place was substituted a series of outcome goals for a variety of different problems and patients. The center would attempt to be less grandiose in its ambition to have an impact upon the overall community. Program staff members have become usefully involved in objectives-setting discussions with funding agencies and community representatives. The author hopes to increase the participation of consumers (e.g., clients and ex-clients) in these discussions.

Cicchinelli, Louis F. PROGRAM EVALUATION RESOURCE CENTER, HENNEPIN COUNTY MENTAL HEALTH SERVICE, MINNEAPOLIS, MINNESOTA. Evaluation Unit Profile, no. 2. Denver: University of Denver, Research Institute, Center for Social Research and Development, March 1977. 50 p.

> This profile, part of an excellent series, indicates that users of goal attainment scaling are requesting more standardization in both goal statement definitions and in goal-setting procedures. Standardization, potentially involving a loss of flexibility, may depend upon the specificity of the agency mission, the homogeneity of the client population, and the treatment techniques employed.

Davis, Howard, ed. FOUR WAYS TO GOAL ATTAINMENT: EVALUATION. Special Monograph no. 1, n.d. 28 p.

> This monograph presents four articles on four separate goal at-
> tainment procedures. Theodor Bonstedt at Rollman Psychiatric
> Institute in Cincinnati describes concrete goal-setting, a com-
> paratively simple system which shifts the evaluative focus from
> abstract constructs of the total personality to concrete descrip-
> tion of behavioral events. Richard H. Ellis and Nancy Wilson
> at the Fort Logan Mental Health Center detail the goal-oriented
> automated progress note approach, using 703 goal statements
> grouped by domains (medical, symptom, self-concept, patient-
> initiated interaction, and disposition plan). Thomas Kiresuk
> describes goal attainment scaling, and Gilbert Honigfeld and
> Donald F. Klein of Hillside Hospital in Glen Oaks, New York,
> write about the Patient Progress Record, which features computer
> print-out specially tailored questions for therapist use, based
> upon ratings appearing on computerized "fever charts." Howard
> Davis compares and discusses the four models.

Dean, Edwin R. THE CHALLENGE AHEAD: EQUAL OPPORTUNITY IN RE-
FERRAL UNIONS. Washington, D.C.: U.S. Commission on Civil Rights, May
1976. 291 p.

> This study reviews the role that imposed construction compliance
> plans and voluntary hometown plans play in securing employment
> opportunities for minorities and women. To do so, it examines
> the demographic make-up of referral unions, as well as the
> effects of their institutional practices, and it assesses the effec-
> tiveness of federal apprenticeship and journeyman Outreach pro-
> grams. The study recommends that present arrangements be scrapped
> and that both federal contractors and the referral unions with
> whom they have collective bargaining agreements file affirmative
> action plans. Goals and timetables, it states, should be de-
> veloped for each public and private project, as well as for all
> projects.

Deegan, Arthur X., and Fritz, Roger J. MBO GOES TO COLLEGE. Boulder:
University of Colorado, Center for Management and Technical Programs, April
1975. 286 p.

> This is a useful compilation of the lectures and exercises em-
> ployed by the authors in their MBO training sessions. There is
> early instruction, for instance, in the definition of institutional
> purpose. Goals are defined as the amount and direction of
> change desired from the present in a given period of time.
> Needs self-assessment procedures are outlined. A variety of
> goals-setting approaches are outlined, and a decision theory-
> style problem-solving model is introduced.

Delaware. State Department of Public Instruction. DELAWARE EDUCATIONAL ACCOUNTABILITY SYSTEM. Dover: 1973. 6 p.

> The DEAS features three "Rs": results, responsibilities, and revisions. Revisions refer to changes in instruction designed to help students attain more objectives. A goal (one of nine) of having each student develop the "skills needed to understand and express ideas through words, numbers, and other symbols" includes a subgoal (one of fifty-nine) stating that "each student should develop reading skills adequate for him to comprehend books, newspapers, and magazines." A specific objective to help effectuate this subgoal is "Each student should have the ability, by the time he leaves school, to read at the eighth-grade level and comprehend at least 75 to 80 percent of reading material of controlled difficulty."

DeMont, Roger A., and DeMont, Billie. "Educational Accountability and Professional Development: Conflict with Institutional Values." PLANNING AND CHANGING 8 (Summer 1977): 115-25.

> The authors challenge two assumptions: that the additive results of individual accountability efforts lead to institutional accountability; and that such an achievement leads to professionalization of education. The professional development thrust (e.g., teacher centers) should help teachers move beyond institutional expectations to individual selection, articulation, and realization of educational values and roles.

De Sio, Joseph E., and Higgins, John E., Jr. "The Management and Control of Case Handling, Office of the General Council, NLRB." BUREAUCRAT 2 (Winter 1974): 385-94.

> Since case processing goals run the risk of infringing upon the rights of parties in the cases, the agency administers time objectives for handling various stages of the cases. This has proven to be an approach typical of the productivity monitoring efforts of a great many public agencies fulfilling regulatory functions.

Deutscher, Irwin. "Toward Avoiding the Goal Trap in Evaluation Research." In READINGS IN EVALUATION RESEARCH, edited by Francis G. Caro, chapter 14. 2d ed. New York: Russell Sage Foundation, 1977.

> The author suggests that the goals of organizations vary in fact from their descriptions in form. Program administrators may act flexibly, may not articulate what they really want to do in order to better accommodate funding sources, or may want to function in a goal-unspecific manner (to make the sick healthy or the ignorant wise). Official goals may only represent political compromises. The article proposes that evaluators examine what is happening (ongoing process) instead of what happened; search

for unintended consequences; and negotiate reasonable goals and
reasonable methods for assessing them.

DeWoolfson, Bruce M., Jr. "Public Sector MBO and PPB: Cross Fertilization
in Management Systems." PUBLIC ADMINISTRATION REVIEW 35 (July-August
1975): 387-95.

> This gem of an article neatly sorts out the seeming inconsisten-
> cies of purpose of program and issue analysis and MBO. While
> Odiorne in theory and Ukeles in application have effectively
> bridged these gaps, the author details the organizational en-
> vironmental characteristics which, for example, led federal
> PPBS analysts to resist Nixon administration MBO inplementation
> efforts, and business administration-trained MBO staff people to
> be insensitive to the decision-making requirements of the ana-
> lysts. The author successfully makes the case that the procedures
> can effectively be employed in tandem.

Dick, Karl V., and Rettew, Philip L. A STRUCTURED APPROACH TO PRO-
GRAM EVALUATION. Columbus, Ohio: VITA Treatment Center, n.d. 11 p.

> Goal achievement procedures are employed in evaluating the
> progress of seventy-four addicts in a methadone program. Many
> of the patients became invested in the goal attainment approach,
> and it spurred their participation in the program.

Dinkel, John J., and Erickson, Joyce E. "Multiple Objectives in Environmental Protection Programs." POLICY SCIENCES 9 (February 1978): 87-96.

> The authors feel that control agency (law enforcement, environ-
> mental protection, fire prevention, public health) program func-
> tions might best be carried out consistent with multiple objec-
> tives and multidimensional criteria (rather than with a single
> criterion). Conflicts might be addressed through the analysis
> of tradeoffs. This approach would offer a vector, rather than
> scalar, description of program inputs and outputs.

Dowd, E. Thomas, and Kelly, F. Donald. "The Use of Goal Attainment Scaling
in Single Case Research." GOAL ATTAINMENT REVIEW 2 (1975): 11-22.

> Florida State University's Counseling and Guidance Clinic bene-
> fited from the application of goal attainment procedures in two
> respects. Staff members were encouraged to emphasize outcome
> variables in their interviewing as well as process techniques such
> as reflection and confrontation. Focusing on one primary strategy
> for each session helped to generate more forward motion in
> counseling.

Downs, Anthony. "Moving Toward Realistic Housing Goals." In AGENDA
FOR THE NATION, edited by Kermit Gordon. Garden City, N.Y.: Double-
day, 1969. Paperbound.

Perhaps the nation's most famous goal was established in the Housing Act of 1949: ". . . a decent home and a suitable living environment for every American family." This chapter discusses whether the quantitative targets subsequently set by Congress to carry out this objective represent a reasonable estimate of the nation's needs, and describes what public and private sector actions are required to fulfill the objective.

Drucker, Peter F. "MBO--Tool or Master?" FEDERAL ACCOUNTANT 24 (September 1975): 23-29.

In a talk before a group of accountants, the speaker notes that he has advocated management by both objectives and self-control, and that understanding (of co-workers' views) is as important a benefit from MBO as performance. In fact, staff disagreement should be encouraged in the objectives-setting process. The ultimate objectives questions are: What do you do that justifies your being on the payroll? What do you do that we should hold you accountable for by way of contribution? Over what time period?

_____. THE PRACTICE OF MANAGEMENT. New York: Harper and Row, 1954. 404 p.

The author, in this famous reference, discusses the fallacy of the "single objective," and argues that objectives should be fashioned in every area where performance and results directly and vitally affect the survival and prosperity of the organization. The balancing of multiple objectives is a pivotal management strategy responsibility. The involvement of subunit managers in MBO is not merely good human relations participatory process, but also the real test of their managerial judgment. Further self-control leads to stronger motivation, and review by superiors of agreed-upon measures of performance is an advantageous managerial control model: Managers don't take action only because someone has told them what to do; they take action because the objective needs of tasks require it. See particularly chapter 7: "The Objectives of a Business" and chapter 11: "Management by Objectives and Self-Control."

_____. "What Results Should You Expect? A Users' Guide to MBO." PUBLIC ADMINISTRATION REVIEW 36 (January-February 1976): 12-19.

The author finds that the politically self-conscious inclination of government to define motherhood objectives is indicative of the problem of securing measurable results from public programs. He proposes that government engage in more rigorous definition of its functions, and, for example, consider the "abandonment of yesterday." He comments that if there were transportation ministeries in 1900, they would have been developing programs to reeducate the horse. Measurement, a difficult process, should be reserved for questions of outcome or effectiveness.

Educational Policy Research Center. ACCOUNTABILITY IN EDUCATION. Research memorandum 6747-15. Menlo Park, Calif.: Stanford Research Institute, 1972. 81 p.

> Accountability is described as a process whose products might include: (1) enhanced performance incentives through feedback and competition; (2) increased local quality control; and (3) increased knowledge about the mechanics of the learning process. This monograph explores the concepts and issues involved in the accountability discussion, laying out some controversial propositions as it does so. For example, teacher accountability fails to fulfill the conditions the center lays out. Teachers lack the necessary power to make the decisions and changes they feel necessary to teach effectively. The absence of incentives further undermines the feasibility of assigning responsibility on that level.

Endicott, Jean; Spitzer, Robert L.; Fleiss, Joseph L.; and Cohen, Jacob. "The Global Assessment Scale: A Procedure for Measuring Overall Severity of Psychiatric Disturbance." ARCHIVES OF GENERAL PSYCHIATRY 33 (June 1976): 766-71.

> The Global Assessment Scale is one of a variety of rating scales of overall severity of illness, which are useful in measuring change. Most scales have five or seven points marked with single-word adjectives but without any cues or criteria to aid the rater. It is, of course, difficult to choose the right wording for these cues:
> e.g., 100 No symptoms, superior functioning in a wide range of activities, life's problems never seem to
> 91 get out of hand, is sought out by others because of his warmth and integrity.
> or: 80 Minimal symptoms may be present but no more than slight impairment in functioning, varying degrees
> 71 of everyday worries and problems that sometimes get out of hand.

"Equal Employment: Opportunity or Quota?" Proceedings of Conference held 6 June 1973, in New York City. CONFERENCE BOARD RECORD 10 (August 1973): 46-61.

> C. Paul Sparks writes that the ultimate goal of parity in the entire work force for minorities and women must be achieved by goals tied to timetables, but worries that conciliation efforts might be resolved by quotas. Kenneth Clark recalls 1963 demonstrations against all-white construction crews in Harlem, and the denunciations the demonstrations engendered from the press and political leadership. William Brown writes about the failure of corporations to assume responsibilities on a voluntary basis, the reason for a regulatory system designed to measure performance.

Etzel, Michael J., and Ivancevich, John M. "Management by Objectives in Marketing: Philosophy, Process, and Problems." JOURNAL OF MARKETING 38 (October 1974): 47-55.

The authors provide a clear description of MBO concepts generally, and a case study, complete with evaluation forms, details a marketing application of the process. There is useful
discussion of such possible implementation difficulties as limited
top level support, the absence of manuals and explanatory forms,
time lag in institutionalization, and requirements to provide
feedback and support to subordinates.

Fleming, John E.; Gill, Gerald R.; and Swinton, David H. THE CASE FOR
AFFIRMATIVE ACTION FOR BLACKS IN HIGHER EDUCATION. Washington,
D.C.: Howard University Press, 1978. 416 p.

This is a large briefing book on the issue drafted by the Institute
for the Study of Educational Policy at Howard. There are extensive descriptive discussions of the goals and timetables approach, as well as a series of case studies--Harvard, Florida
State, and Oberlin and Merritt Colleges.

Forehand, Garlie A.; Marco, Gary L.; McDonald, Frederick J.; Murphy, Richard
T.; and Quirk, Thomas J. AN ACCOUNTABILITY DESIGN FOR SCHOOL
SYSTEMS. Research bulletin RB-73-38. Princeton, N.J.: Educational Testing
Service, June 1973. 50 p. Paperbound.

The authors detail a comprehensive plan for elementary and
secondary school accountability. Functional performance analysis
is organized around the determination of how many students score
below minimum standards, and around a Student Development
Index, a deviation measure of performance based upon longitudinal student data. Key process variables are then identified
for policy review.

Frank, Edward. "Motivation by Objectives--A Case Study." RESEARCH MAN-
AGEMENT 12 (November 1969): 391-400.

This application of the approach focused more upon organization
and self-motivation than upon control or performance evaluation.
Somewhat reticent and individualistic scientists improved their
skills in communicating their plans, hopes, and aspirations. The
newest staff members were particularly supportive since they felt
that greater responsibility might be delegated to them, and they
might assume more in the way of decision-making roles.

Freedman, Jay; Gordus, Jeanne; Kirkhart, Karen; and Overgerger, Carla. BE-
YOND CRAFT: USING WHAT YOU KNOW. Ann Arbor: University of Michigan,
School of Social Work Continuing Education Program in the Human Services,
1977. 17 p.

Project CRAFT provides a series of self-awareness exercises in
individual professional goal development for child placement
workers. Readers are asked to define assessment, placement,
and/or maintenance and change problems in their direct practice,

interagency, intraagency, and community outreach activities. Scaling procedures are demonstrated for the review of goals. Measurement and results concepts are also featured.

Freeman, Leslie. "Innovations in Compliance: The Legal Aid Society of Alameda County Monitors Affirmative Action." CIVIL RIGHTS DIGEST 10 (Summer 1978): 21-27.

> The Legal Aid Society of Alameda County developed a community-based monitoring system to review the success of local businesses in meeting the goals and timetables of their affirmative action plans. After securing the plans and work force data under the Freedom of Information Act from federal compliance offices, they themselves conducted the underutilization analyses needed to validate the goal projections.

French, Wendell L.; and Hollmann, Robert W. "Management by Objectives: The Team Approach." CALIFORNIA MANAGEMENT REVIEW 17 (Spring 1975): 13-22.

> The authors urge implementation of Collaborative MBO, because they feel that organizational success often results from inter-dependent efforts (horizontally, vertically, or diagonally). Superiors functioning as central processing centers of objectives miss opportunities for coordination of objectives and operations. Particularly difficult are integrative relationships in objectives-setting between different functional arms of the organization (e.g., production and marketing).

Fri, Robert W. "How to Manage the Government for Results: The Rise of MBO." ORGANIZATIONAL DYNAMICS 2 (Spring 1974): 19-33.

> The author proposes that federal efforts should neither focus on the budget nor become preoccupied with accounting structures. Management leaders, not staffs, should be responsible for setting objectives. Actions, rather than plans, should be the target of MBO efforts, and units should develop their own systems, keeping the systems as simple as possible. Responsibility-accounting structures should be built around line managers, and carried out through cost, rather than fiscal accounting.

Froomkin, Joseph. "Needed: A New Framework for the Analysis of Government Programs." POLICY ANALYSIS 2 (Spring 1976): 341-50.

> The writer argues that evaluation should not be limited to stated objectives of programs. Title I educational programs, for example, may have, in addition to their stated objectives, also increased the employment of teachers when the supply of teachers was tight, and reduced the size of classes in central city areas. Higher education subsidies have been effective in expanding opportunities, but other positive consequences have included

reductions in high school dropout rates among some groups, and income distributional changes between skilled workers and college graduates not practicing law or medicine. Cost estimation of program objectives is limited to target groups, although there may be pressure to spread program benefits to other groups as well.

Garwick, Geoffrey. COMBINING SHORT-TERM AND LONG-TERM GOALS. Minneapolis, Minn.: Program Evaluation Resource Center, October 1975. 50 p.

This report illustrates a possible goal attainment scaling approach to combining the future-oriented perspective of long-term goals (e.g., post-treatment resocialization) with the quick changes and immediacy of short-term goals. The paper discusses how to conceptualize gradual approximations to long-term goals, how to abandon an unnecessary or harmful short-term goal, and how to relate many short-term goals to a single long-term goal. New forms and schematics are provided to demonstrate these procedures.

_____. "A Construct Validity Overview of Goal Attainment Scaling." In PROGRAM EVALUATION PROJECT REPORT, 1969-1973, chapter 5. Minneapolis, Minn.: Program Evaluation Resource Center, June 1974.

While the basic construct underlying goal attainment scaling is "attainment of expectations," it is accompanied by many other variables related to the many possible ways in which the approach can be applied. This report lists these variables and a system for illustrating hypotheses. The findings support the original Kiresuk-Sherman hypotheses (see p. 113).

_____. "Defining and Validating Goal Attainment Scaling." GOAL ATTAINMENT REVIEW 2 (1975): 1-10.

Because the approach's proponents believe that its mere use does not necessarily result in easily interpretable results, and its design is crucial to the utility of its findings, six features are proposed to define the procedure: (1) tailor-made, client-specific scales, based upon the particular abilities, history, and problems of the client; (2) goals that focus on the future and show targets to be achieved; (3) specificity; (4) the realism of the expected level at the center of the scale; (5) polychotomous scales; and (6) systematic enumeration, allowing a summary value for each set of scales, regardless of the diversity of the variables included.

_____. INTRODUCTION TO GOAL ATTAINMENT SCALING. 3 pts. Minneapolis, Minn.: Program Evaluation Resource Center, February 1973. Part 1: 23 p.; Part 2: 25 p.; Part 3: 22 p.

The lecture transcript in Part 1 discusses procedures: weighing of problem areas to show relative importance; selection of specific variables to indicate progress for each problem area; selection of a specific set of expectations of outcome for each variable; and the use of realistic expectations, rather than only emphasizing change. Part 2 addresses the need for other outcome measurement and for consumer satisfaction surveying. Common difficulties are highlighted: vagueness, multiple variables, the selection of variables to measure problem areas, and follow-up guide construction. Part 3 lays out a practice case, discusses reliability and validity, and proposes that feedback, joint planning, and clarity are necessary in a program evaluation system.

_____. "An Introduction to Reliability and the Goal Attainment Scaling Methodology." In PROGRAM EVALUATION PROJECT REPORT, 1969-1973, chapter 3. Minneapolis, Minn.: Program Evaluation Resource Center, June 1974.

Since reliability is considered to be a basic aspect of a measurement system, this report discusses the theory underlying applications of conventional reliability concepts to goal attainment scaling, and reviews a range of studies relevant to the reliability of the methodology. Follow-up guide construction and follow-up guide scoring are the two types of reliability issues discussed.

General Electric. GENERAL ELECTRIC'S COMMITMENT TO PROGRESS IN EQUAL OPPORTUNITY AND MINORITY RELATIONS. New York: August 1970. 42 p.

This is a case study depicting the organizational process employed by General Electric to develop central management's view of goals and objectives in this field. Task forces were assigned to analyze the environment, define the corporate role, and assess business opportunities relevant to minority relations. Their recommendations are summarized, and a draft is presented of the measurement format designed to account for progress on unit-derived goals and objectives. The case demonstrates how an Equal Employment Opportunity affirmative action plan can be integrated within a corporate MBO planning approach.

Giegold, William C. "MBO After All These Years: Just Another Flash in the Pan?" CONFERENCE BOARD RECORD 12 (July 1975): 49-52.

Prerequisites for introducing MBO successfully include a well-thought-out organizational structure in which responsibilities and areas of authority are clearly spelled out and understood, a heavy commitment to improved effectiveness on the part of higher management, an organizational climate in which interfunctional communication is an accepted way of life, and the ability of managers and employees to communicate productively with one another. Any organization so well off is one which is least likely to need MBO, and least likely to see any effects as a result of its introduction.

Gillings, Dennis. EVALUATION: A METHODOLOGY FOR DETERMINING THE EFFECTIVENESS OF A SOCIAL PROGRAM IN TERMS OF GOAL FULFILL-MENT. Chapel Hill: University of North Carolina, School of Public Health, October 1972. 51 p. Tables.

> A goal-centered program evaluation methodology is delineated, focusing on the appropriate perspective to take in measuring performance targets, across periods of program activity during which objectives may be modified. A case study is presented, describing the evaluation of the Lincoln Community Health Center. A series of tables show the performance data collected for the project.

Gillings, Dennis, and Fisher, Gail. SOME STATISTICAL METHODS IN EVAL-UATION. Paper presented at the Joint Meeting of the Biometric Society, I.M.S., and A.S.A. at Ithaca, New York, 30 May-1 June 1973. Chapel Hill: University of North Carolina, School of Public Health, 1973. 19 p.

> Objectives should be understood to involve activity (the work to be done), and target (how much work is to be done by when). Evaluation should examine: (1) achievement, the degree to which objectives are fulfilled; (2) effectiveness, the degree to which goals are fulfilled; (3) efficiency, the degree to which achievement is maximized relative to resources available; (4) balance, the degree to which the first three attributes are uniform over the various areas of concern consistent with program priorities; (5) adequacy, the degree to which the allocated resources match the need; (6) consistency, the degree to which the first five attributes are maintained over time; and (7) appropriateness, the degree to which a program, in relation to programs with overlapping concerns, is optimal in regard to meeting the mission of the program. Procedures are proposed to evaluate objectives of each of these seven types.

Glasner, Daniel M. "Patterns of Management by Results: A New Classification Scheme." BUSINESS HORIZONS 12 (February 1969): 37-40.

> This article classifies patterns of management. Task management, effective in emergencies, involves assignment of specific tasks to subordinates. Job management is defined as the selection of individuals to fulfill job description sets of responsibilities, which they then are left free to carry out. Man-job management is a pattern within which managers and subordinates share an understanding of work, and in which they meet for periodic reviews. Goals-oriented management is differentiated from accountability by the addition, in the latter case, of joint efforts to both set goals in terms of levels measurement (rather than only in terms of need) and define methods of measurement to assess accomplishment.

Glazer, Nathan. AFFIRMATIVE DISCRIMINATION: ETHNIC INEQUALITY
AND PUBLIC POLICY. New York: Basic Books, 1975. 248 p.

> The author contends that the federal governmental shift in policy
> emphasis from opportunities to results (goals and timetables) may
> be tolerable only if one views minority group social conditions
> to be very poor; feels that racism is deeply institutionalized;
> and believes that affirmative action can effectively alleviate
> some of the worst conditions. See particularly chapters 2 and
> 6.

Glendenning, James W., and Bullock, R.E.H. MANAGEMENT BY OBJEC-
TIVES IN LOCAL GOVERNMENT. London: Charles Knight and Co., 1973.
255 p.

> The Local Government Training Board commissioned consultants
> to introduce MBO to a county architect's office, a clerk's de-
> partment, and an education department. The authors find that
> these agencies did in fact become more action-oriented and
> focused on the quality and promptness of results, rather than
> upon the administrative input which is required. Delegation
> increased and became more effective. Teamwork was promoted
> at the same time that individual accountability for results was
> clarified. The three case histories are presented in detail.

Goetz, Billy E. "The Management of Objectives." MANAGEMENT ACCOUNT-
ING 55 (August 1973): 35-38.

> MBO profit centers in private industry, while assuring motivation,
> may encourage suboptimization and inter-unit conflict (e.g.,
> over transfer prices). A better approach would focus on the
> need for managers to encourage the cooperation of people like
> stockholders, leaders, suppliers, and customers. All of these
> individuals will need to have their own objectives met. Ob-
> jectives should be costed to determine how best to manage at
> the margin. In such ways, management of objectives, a plan-
> ning process, can guide management by objectives, a control
> mechanism.

Goltz, Barbara; Rusk, Thomas N.; and Sternbach, Richard A. "A Built-in
Evaluation System in a New Community Mental Health Program." AMERICAN
JOURNAL OF PUBLIC HEALTH 63 (August 1973): 702-9.

> The article describes the behavioral goal development process
> negotiated between clients and program staff members. When
> the two individuals meet to evaluate progress, the client may
> be biased, either merely expressing satisfaction, or trying to
> please or draw the attention of the staff members. However,
> this joint assessment helps draw out discussion of difficulties,
> and provides positive feedback, when appropriate.

Greenhill, Muriel, ed. THEORY/PRACTICE CURRICULUM IN PUBLIC ADMIN-
ISTRATION. Brooklyn N.Y.: Medgar Evers College, Institute of Public Administration, 1978. C.B.A. 4 Unit C: 23 p.

> This is a series of materials detailing personnel procedures and
> approaches under New York City's management (MBO) plan.
> Included is a case study which details how the fire department
> solves a series of problems in order to attain their goals.

Hall, James N., and Mathison, Mansel T. "Adaptation of Goal Attainment
Scaling to an Outpatient Drug Treatment Program." GOAL ATTAINMENT
REVIEW 2 (1975): 109-15.

> As administrators of a prescriptive drug treatment multiservice
> center, the authors adopted goal attainment procedures which
> allowed for evaluation consistent with the eclectic philosophy
> of the agency. A case manager would construct or work out
> with a client a minimum of three treatment goals during the
> client's first two weeks with the agency. The agency is pleased
> with the planning focus this procedure forces upon its staff members.
> Additionally, a false success versus failure dichotomy can be
> avoided. An implementation problem has been staff difficulty
> in properly drafting goals (e.g., overlapping levels of perfor-
> mance, vagueness, and including more than one variable in a
> goal in which the variables might be affected in opposite direc-
> tions).

Hancock, Cyril J. "MBO in the Government Service: The First Five Years."
MANAGEMENT SERVICES IN GOVERNMENT 29 (February 1974): 16-26.

> The British treasury department reports its experience, derived
> from thirty-nine projects, involving 12,250 managers. Recom-
> mendations focus on securing the support of top management,
> committing junior managers to involve their operating staffs in
> developing objectives and suggestions for improvements, and
> associating changes with long-term improvements in individual
> and organizational effectiveness.

Havemann, Joel. "Executive Report/Ford Endorses 172 Goals of 'Management
by Objective' Plan." NATIONAL JOURNAL REPORTS 6 (26 October 1974):
1597-1605.

> Transition from the Nixon to the Ford administration leads to
> changes in the MBO process: the volume of objectives is to be
> reduced to a number in which the president can have direct
> interest, and OMB can keep track of. Management conferences
> are to be scheduled only on request. Among the 172 listed
> presidential objectives, the leading topic is the economy and
> business.

_____. "Nixon Approves 144 Agency Goals, OMB Begins Program to Coordinate Policy." NATIONAL JOURNAL REPORTS 5 (17 November 1973): 1703-09.

As the presidential objectives are defined, the Office of Management and Budget moves into the tracking phase of its MBO
program--bimonthly progress report meetings with the agencies.
There are twenty-two business and economy objectives, eighteen
energy objectives, seventeen environmental objectives, and one
educational objective. Some administrators express enthusiasm
for the opportunity to offer feedback to OMB.

_____. "OMB Begins Major Program to Identify and Attain Presidential Goals."
NATIONAL JOURNAL REPORTS 5 (2 June 1973): 783-95.

As the Nixon administration adopts MBO, Roy Ash at OMB
states that MBO will absorb the budget cycle. The author
notes that necessary but poorly quantified goals may be rele-
gated aside. Agencies are asked to define their own objectives, although they initially fear that OMB or the White House
will impose their own preferences. MBO is discussed from the
point of view of each of the cabinet departments.

_____. "OMB's 'Management By Objective' Produces Goals of Uneven Quality."
NATIONAL JOURNAL REPORTS 5 (18 August 1973): 1201-10.

The writer criticizes some of the first round of federal energy
and natural resources objectives as too vague. Others, he finds,
evaluate process, rather than outcome. Environmental goals
stated in the State of the Union message are not included. The
article describes an OMB-Department of the Interior meeting to
set objectives.

Havens, Harry S. "MBO and Program Evaluation, or Whatever Happened to
PPBS?" PUBLIC ADMINISTRATION REVIEW 36 (January-February 1976): 40-
45.

The author contends that federal MBO implementation will be
difficult, given the nature of policy decisions, the character of
the decision-making process, and the limitations in regard to
the quantifying of goals. He comments that the appearance of
neatness cannot create the fact of rationality. Sometimes, programs are established, for example, to demonstrate concern about
a problem, without hope of solving that problem. Decisions may
be purposefully fuzzy (all things to all people) to respond to a
concensus, rather than to the needs of a staff member formalizing
goal statements. Since MBO forces officials to think about
their purposes, the approach may be of some help.

Hawthorne, Phyllis. LEGISLATION BY THE STATES: ACCOUNTABILITY AND
ASSESSMENT IN EDUCATION. Denver: Cooperative Accountability Project,
April 1973. 91 p.

This compendium of legislation includes fall 1972 summaries of progress: twenty-three states with legislation enacted; eight states requiring evaluation of professional employees; and eighteen states with statewide testing or assessment programs.

Hegion, Ada; Fish, Enrica; and Grace, Susan. "Goal Attainment Scaling: An Alternative Technique for Measuring Academic Progress." GOAL ATTAINMENT REVIEW 1 (1974): 20-34.

This application of the procedure, introduced in the Minneapolis schools, requires knowledge of each child's academic strengths and weaknesses, knowledge of response to instructional methods, and precise knowledge of instructional material taught in the classroom and presented in tutoring sessions. Like diagnostic-prescriptive testing approaches, the process is very time-consuming, particularly in terms of the time it takes to construct follow-up guides. Eight pages of examples of goals are presented, as well as three pages of sample follow-up guides.

Henderson, Richard I. "MBO: How it Works in a Sales Force." SUPERVISORY MANAGEMENT 20 (April 1975): 9-14.

CIBA Pharmaceutical Corp. has found that sales units should never have more than three goals, and that the definition of attainment steps is as important as goals definition itself. Reviews are unthreatening, and entirely supportive (e.g., helping salesmen to learn about the "big picture"). This brief article is a rarity in that it actually describes an operational MBO system which other organizations might want to replicate.

Hill, Herbert. LABOR UNION CONTROL OF JOB TRAINING: A CRITICAL ANALYSIS OF APPRENTICESHIP OUTREACH PROGRAMS AND THE HOMETOWN PLANS. Occasional paper 2:1. Washington, D.C.: Howard University, Institute for Urban Affairs and Research, 1974. 129 p.

This report traces the progress of the Philadelphia Plan and other hometown plans, which it describes as establishing the legality of the use of specific numbers in civil rights law enforcement. The author finds voluntarism to be an inadequate substitute for governmental enforcement of the civil rights laws.

Hodgson, J.S. "Management by Objectives--The Experience of a Federal Government Department." CANADIAN PUBLIC ADMINISTRATION 16 (Fall 1973): 422-31.

The Canadian deputy minister of veterans affairs argues for MBO as part of an overall organizational development process. He suggests an implementation procedure involving preliminary research by a senior official; senior staff participation in a "concept clarification seminar"; follow-up review sessions; the drafting of a statement of continuing departmental objectives; adoption of goals by the key program administrators; and the recruitment and training of two dozen middle management MBO advisors.

Horton, Gerald T.; Anderson, Eugene D.; Corish, Thomas K.; and Gottlieb, Joel I. GOAL AND OBJECTIVE SETTING IN A TITLE XX STATE SOCIAL SERVICES PLANNING SYSTEM. Atlanta: Research Group, April 1975. 36 p.

This is a social services planning manual filled with examples, sample forms, and explanatory information concerning five concepts: national goals; service and administrative objectives; alignment of services and objectives to national goals; fiscal year and annual objectives; and objectives for monitoring and evaluation.

House, Ernest; Rivers, Wendell; and Stufflebeam, Daniel L. "An Assessment of the Michigan Accountability System." PHI DELTA KAPPAN 55 (June 1974): 663-69.

This article represents the counterattack on Michigan's state accountability model. The authors attack the claim that the model's objectives reflect consensus on the definition of what minimal performance should be expected. The results of the application of the unvalidated objectives-referenced tests indicated that not a single school district in the state was meeting "minimal" objectives in mathematics and reading. The authors argue that Michigan is unwise to tie test results to state compensatory education funding levels to localities. They also suggest that state-developed objectives should not necessarily be substituted for locally developed objectives.

Houts, Peter S., and Scott, Robert A. "Goal Planning in Mental Health Rehabilitation." GOAL ATTAINMENT REVIEW 2 (1975): 33-51.

This article describes the authors' project applying David McClelland's work on training achievement motivation strategies to the needs of a severely handicapped group often described as lacking in motivation and mental patients with histories of long-term hospitalization for mental illness. McClelland's concepts of achievement motivation behaviors include setting reasonable goals; developing plans for achieving these goals, adjusting goals and plans based on experience, and a high degree of commitment and involvement in working toward goals. The project decided additionally to focus on patients' strengths rather than problems, to train staff rather than patients themselves, and to use goal planning rather than achievement motivation as a more accessible title for their efforts.

_____. GOAL PLANNING WITH DEVELOPMENTALLY DISABLED PERSONS: PROCEDURES FOR DEVELOPING AN INDIVIDUALIZED CLIENT PLAN. Hershey: Pennsylvania State University College of Medicine, Department of Behavioral Science, 1975. 103 p.

This manual lays out in popular form five training sessions of instruction in developing individualized client plans. The first session materials include case data, and the later sessions are designed to use participants' own case information. Each set of presentation materials includes charts, forms, and cartoons.

Howe, Clifford E., and Fitzgerald, Marigail E. A MODEL FOR EVALUATING SPECIAL EDUCATION PROGRAMS IN IOWA AREA EDUCATION AGENCIES. Iowa City: University of Iowa, June 1976. 50 p.

This manual outlines a field-tested model to be used by the State Division of Special Education and Area Education Agency Directors of Special Education. MBO formats are offered for Level II middle managers (e.g., in regard to an autism grant) and teachers (Level III) are asked to use goal attainment scales (for which numerous examples are also provided).

Howell, Robert A. "A Fresh Look at Management by Objectives." BUSINESS HORIZONS 10 (Fall 1967): 51-58.

The author focuses on the top-level management role in MBO in this influential article. He urges organization-wide dissemination of management's goals, followed by bottom-up individual formulation of objectives, and lateral trade-offs determined by peer groups reviewing the objectives of their colleagues. The article broke ground in arguing that benefits might accrue most significantly for the overall organization, as well as for individuals, and personnel officers. Consequently, MBO as a management control and planning system, should involve the same kinds of trade-off analyses as are undertaken in the budget process.

Ivancevich, John M. "A Longitudinal Assessment of Management by Objectives." ADMINISTRATIVE SCIENCE QUARTERLY 17 (March 1972): 126-38.

The author studied implementation by a top management cadre at a supply firm, compared against personnel department implementation at a manufacturing company. In both companies, he finds inadequate reinforcement of commitment to the process after training, and that, without this, the effects of training, if any, are diluted or eliminated completely.

_____. "The Theory and Practice of Management by Objectives." MICHIGAN BUSINESS REVIEW 21 (March 1969): 13-16.

In this earlier report by the author on his MBO research at two companies, he finds lower-level managers at one of the firms to be out of the mainstream of the process with no enhancement of their self-actualization, esteem, or security. Often their superiors were said to be unenthusiastic about the approach. In the other firm, with more active higher-level support, lower-level managers were found to feel more secure, and pleased to be participating as an active part of the management team. Objections were expressed about the difficulty of quantifying goals.

"Job Discrimination and Affirmative Action." CIVIL RIGHTS DIGEST 7 (Spring 1975): entire issue.

This special fifty-six page issue begins with a debate on discrimination in higher education between Miro Todorovich and Howard Glickstein. Glickstein writes, in defense of goals and timetables, that when a society has committed past injustices, it simply is not possible to achieve equality and fairness by applying neutral principles. Alfred and Ruth Blumrosen discuss the seniority issues which occur when affirmative action and layoff agreements conflict, and Willo White write about testing and equal opportunity.

Jun, Jong S. "Management by Objectives in the Public Sector." PUBLIC ADMINISTRATION REVIEW 36 (January-February 1976): 1-5.

The editor of this journal's symposium points out that MBO has been simultaneously confusing and stimulating for public administrators, because, in his view, for the first time, government is adopting a less instrumental and more humane approach to the problems of interface between the person and complex organizations. Shared power and decentralization are two other themes he highlights, and he points out that effective MBO administrators need to have an action, rather than a technique, orientation.

Kasputys, Joseph E., and Anthony, Robert N. U.S. NAVAL SUPPLY CENTER, NEWPORT, R.I. (A), (B) AND (C). Boston: Intercollegiate Case Clearing House, 1972. (A) Case 9-172-602: 25 p.; teaching note 9-172-605: 11 p.

This series of cases is designed to illustrate the use of output measures in nonprofit organizations. The (A) case describes the output measures employed on three separate levels, and the control system organized to evaluate performance. In the (B) case, a new commanding officer utilizes the MBO system to take charge of the organization. Inadequate output measures demonstrate the trade-offs between the motivational and the planning-budgeting uses of the approach.

Kearney, C. Philip. "The Politics of Educational Assessment in Michigan." PLANNING AND CHANGING 1 (July 1970): 71-82.

The article describes the political events surrounding the development of Michigan's educational accountability process. In one of the great understatements, Kearney notes that the process is intricately complex and one that does not necessarily end with the passage of legislation.

Kennedy, Jill, and Fletcher, John E., Jr., eds. EEO AND THE CITIES. Transcript of a workshop at the Congress of Cities in San Juan, 4 December 1973. Washington, D.C.: National League-U.S. Conference of Mayors, July 1974. 154 p.

> Mayor Richard H. Marriott of Sacramento discusses the impact upon cities of being included within the federal enforcement system. Thomas Cody describes affirmation action in terms of its emphasis upon results. Irving Kator discusses the relationship of merit objectives to EEO objectives. Other speakers include a municipal attorney, a state personnel director, and Eleanor Holmes Norton, who administers the U.S. Equal Employment Opportunity Commission.

King, Larry W.; Austin, Nancy K.; Liberman, Robert P.; and DeRisi, William J. "Accountability, Like Charity, Begins at Home." EVALUATION 2 (January 1974): 75-77.

> The Behavior Analysis and Modification Project at the Oxnard, California, Community Mental Health Center employed goal attainment scaling to evaluate both treatment outcome, and the activities of the evaluative research project itself.

Kirchhoff, Bruce A. "Using Objectives: The Critical Factor in Effective MBO." MICHIGAN BUSINESS REVIEW 26 (January 1974): 17-21.

> The author reiterates Peter Drucker's admonition to managers to avoid drives. He notes that management development and MBO themselves can be candidates for drives. Managers must learn not only to set objectives, but also how to use these objectives within their own operational contexts.

Kiresuk, Thomas J., and Garwick, Geoffrey. "Basic Goal Attainment Scaling Procedures." In PROGRAM EVALUATION PROJECT REPORT, 1969-1973, chapter 1. Minneapolis, Minn.: Program Evaluation Resource Center, April 1975.

> This section of the evaluation report briefly runs through all of the procedures--designations of and predictions for problem areas, the follow-up interview, the goal attainment score, varieties of scaling.

Kiresuk, Thomas J., and Sherman, Robert E. "Goal Attainment Scaling: A General Method for Evaluating Comprehensive Community Mental Health Programs." COMMUNITY MENTAL HEALTH JOURNAL 4 (June 1968): 443-53.

> This is the founding article of the Goal Attainment Scaling movement. The authors believe that the determination and specification of goals should take place either between patient and therapist, or at the time of the establishment of a contract between the patient and the organization. They propose for the

first time an approach which includes goal selection and scaling; random assignment of the patient to one of the treatment modalities; and the follow-up of each patient with regard to the goals and scale values chosen at intake.

Kivens, Laurence, and Bolin, David C. "Evaluation in a Community Mental Health Center: Hillsborough CMHC, Tampa, Florida." EVALUATION 3 (January-February 1976): 98-105.

This center uses a series of modified goal attainment approaches, such as a "Functioning, Importance, and Goal Success" procedure, and a combination of a Goal-Oriented Automated Progress Note and a Goal Attainment Scale. There is an effort to rate various behavioral attributes by both the level of the patient's functionality and how important he or she feels the behavior to be. Procedures are used more for process purposes than as outcome studies, because the program's director feels that they lack good enough techniques that are reasonably practical and cost-effective and able to document outcome.

Klitgaard, Robert E. ACHIEVEMENT SCORES AND EDUCATIONAL OBJECTIVES. Report R-1217-N.E. Santa Monica, Calif.: Rand Corp., January 1974. 54 p.

This monograph is part of the series developed for the National Institute of Education to assist the Alum Rock, California, tuition voucher demonstration project. It attempts to develop new ways to look at achievement scores as measures of educational outcomes, since they may be the only measures available; even though their underlying objectives may be fuzzy and controversial, and evaluations may implicitly assume that schools with higher average achievement scores are better, implying a simplistic and probably incorrect objective function. The new measures which are proposed are described in detail.

Kogan, Leonard S., and Shyne, Ann W. "Tender-Minded and Tough-Minded Approaches in Evaluative Research." WELFARE IN REVIEW 4 (February 1966): 12-16.

The authors depict this argument over the measurement of the performance of therapy, as a debate between existential therapists, such as Rollo May and Adrian Van Kaam, and the neo-client-centered therapists, such as Carl Rogers, on the one hand, and Watsonian behaviorists and Pavlovians, on the other hand. Experimentalists, trained in conditioning and learning theory, had moved from the laboratory to work with actual patients. The authors present the problems of symptomatic treatment and symptom substitution.

Koontz, Harold. "Making MBO Effective." CALIFORNIA MANAGEMENT REVIEW 20 (Fall 1977): 5-13.

The writer argues that verifiability is the key to successful application. Major advantages are its usefulness in forcing planning and clarifying organizational roles, its help in operationalizing managerial appraisal and providing the best guides and reasons for control, and its role in eliciting commitment. Goals, however, are difficult to set; too often tend to be short-term; may lead to misemphases; and may inaccurately measure performance. There also may be problems of inflexibility, over-reliance on numbers, arbitrariness, and inapplicable standards.

Landers, Jacob. "Accountability and Progress by Nomenclature: Old Ideas in New Bottles." PHI DELTA KAPPAN 53 (April 1973): 539-41.

This public school administrator feels that accountability is important, because it directs attention to the results of the educational process, rather than to its components, because it fixes responsibility for these results, and because it addresses the consequences of no results or poor results. He is concerned that accountability concepts might restrict the aims of education to those which can be most easily measured, rather than those which are most important.

Lasagna, John B. "Make Your MBO Pragmatic." HARVARD BUSINESS REVIEW 49 (November-December 1971): 64-69.

The argument is made here that MBO might well be initially targeted to serve planning and control purposes. Alternatively, if existing evaluation and compensation systems were to be targeted, they might tend to absorb and stymie these efforts. Unfortunately for planning purposes, the article, based upon experiences at Wells Fargo Bank, argues that "good objectives statements should concentrate on 'what' and 'when,' and not 'why' and 'how.'" The bank's organizational development-style approach in fact uses objectives as means toward better managing and not as ends in themselves.

Lefkovitz, Paul M. "Program Evaluation in a Day Treatment Center." GOAL ATTAINMENT REVIEW 1 (1974): 44-48.

The progress of forty-five patients at this Cincinnati mental health center is studied over a six-month period. The study was undertaken to ascertain the overall efficacy of treatment at the agency, to pinpoint strengths and weaknesses, and to aid in treatment planning by facilitating individualized goal-setting and by concretizing therapeutic expectations for each patient.

Lester, Richard A. ANTIBIAS REGULATION OF UNIVERSITIES: FACULTY PROBLEMS AND THEIR SOLUTIONS. New York: McGraw-Hill, 1974. 168 p.

This report, prepared for the Carnegie Commission, details faculty appointment processes, supply and demand conditions, and the federal guidelines which require the development of availability analyses (which the author finds to be inappropriate). In chapter 5, he focuses on goals and timetables and expresses concern about techniques which inflate goals, such as projections based upon the number of Ph.D. holders during a past period, which he says does not account for the amount and quality of their developmental experience during that period. He then proposes his own outline of a federal enforcement approach.

Levinson, Harry. "Management by Objectives: A Critique." TRAINING AND DEVELOPMENT JOURNAL 26 (April 1972): 3-8.

The author argues that interdependence must be taken into account in MBO and that mutual appraisal processes should be developed for bosses and subordinates. Organizational purpose, as well as goals, must be understood, and partnership relationships should be developed to heighten motivation.

_____. "Management by Whose Objectives?" HARVARD BUSINESS REVIEW 48 (July-August 1970): 123-32.

According to the author, when limited to reward-punishment psychology, MBO combined with performance appraisal is self-defeating. The individual's personal goals must be considered first, in terms of what he or she wants from work, and particularly in terms of the relationship of those needs and wants to organizational objectives. Superiors should be freed of responsibility for conducting hostile activities, and subordinates need to be free to evaluate themselves against what needs to be done in an environment which encourages them to solve problems spontaneously.

Lewis, Robert W. "Measuring, Reporting and Appraising Results of Operations with Reference to Goals, Plans, and Budgets." In PLANNING, MANAGING AND MEASURING THE BUSINESS: A CASE STUDY OF MANAGEMENT PLANNING AND CONTROL OF GENERAL ELECTRIC COMPANY, pp. 29-42. New York: Controllership Foundation, January 1955.

Historically, General Electric's MBO approach was based upon unit, rather than individual evaluation, and is used to formulate common indexes of performance, rather than standards. Measurements were developed in terms of operational objectives (e.g., profitability and market position), functional objectives (e.g., engineering, marketing, finance), and managerial objectives (e.g., planning, organizing, integrating). Other operational objectives include productivity, product leadership, personnel development, employee attitudes, public responsibility, and balance between short-range and long-range goals.

Liberman, Robert. BEHAVIORAL GOAL ATTAINMENT--USES IN TREATMENT AND EVALUATION. Minneapolis, Minn.: Program Evaluation Resource Center, September 1975. 29 p.

> Behavior therapy is unthinkable, explains the psychiatrist, without a concurrent system of measurement, such as goal attainment methods. He describes the approach he took in implementing the process at the Oxnard Mental Health Center: asking about the kinds of behavior and clinical problems of real interest to clinicians; determining carefully how much recording is really necessary; and ascertaining the correct pace for implementation. One problem was staff substitution of trivial goals (punctuality, credits earned in the token economy) for more functional goals.

Lurie, Ellen. TRAINING FOR LOCAL CONTROL: CURRICULUM AND AC-COUNTABILITY. Bronx, N.Y.: United Bronx Parents, 1968. 18 p.

> This package of training materials includes state minimum education requirements, city promotion, acceleration and graduation requirements, curriculum standards, the performance data for all junior high schools, academic high schools, and a report card for parents to use in evaluating their schools.

Luthans, Fred. "How to Apply MBO." PUBLIC PERSONNEL MANAGEMENT 5 (March-April 1976): 82-87.

> The author proposes that the translation of MBO to the public sector should occur after the identification of those "environmental variables that have a contingent relationship with the overall concept of MBO." Key to his contingency management approach to MBO, for example, are agreement upon objectives and their measures; and the responsiveness of public organizations to the political climate.

Lynch, Ronald G. MANAGEMENT BY OBJECTIVES. Chapel Hill: University of North Carolina, Institute of Government, 1977. 34 p.

> This is a handy manual which both discusses and charts the implementation of MBO program evaluation procedures: specifying measurable objectives; formulating a practical evaluation design; specifying data collection procedures; and specifying data analysis methods. Examples of and formats for writing objectives, approving projects, and planning project actions are provided.

Lyons Morris, Lynn, and Taylor Fitz-Gibbon, Carol. HOW TO DEAL WITH GOALS AND OBJECTIVES. Beverly Hills, Calif.: Sage Publications, 1978. 78 p.

> This discussion of educational evaluative objectives focuses on some principles involved in developing behavioral objectives; their use in describing ends, not means; the different levels of

skill attainment which are intended; and their use for whole programs, as well as for individuals. An annotated affective do-
main taxonomy is presented illustratively. The relationship of
objectives to standardized tests is discussed, and a chapter on
determining priorities lays out alternative approaches, including
random sampling, combining independent ratings, construction
hierarchies, and matrix sampling.

_____. HOW TO MEASURE ACHIEVEMENT. Beverly Hills, Calif.: Sage
Publications, 1978. 159 p.

This educational testing evaluation primer describes how to determine how well a test fits a program: by refining and classi-
fying objectives, by obtaining and screening test specimens, and
by examining the match of the objectives to the test items.
Other chapters discuss reliability and validity, and the recording
and reporting of data derived from test scores.

McCaffery, Jerry. "MBO and the Federal Budgetary Process." PUBLIC AD-
MINISTRATION REVIEW 36 (January-February 1976): 33-39.

The author suggests that MBO can be used to link the planning
and budgeting processes together because of its own dual focus
upon planning and control. He contrasts MBO with PPBS, by
defining the former as an administrative decision-making mechanism, operating continuously and intermittently aggregating data
for top-level policy choices; and the latter as a policy choice
mechanism, operating periodically, which results in disaggregated
down-the-line managerial decisions. He reports findings from a
series of interviews during the spring of 1975 with southeastern
federal regional administrators.

McCann, Daniel. "MBO: How It Is Structured and Coordinated." SUPER-
VISORY MANAGEMENT 20 (April 1975): 2-8.

The writer argues for a highly structured system which should not
appear to be so. Objectives should not be quickly put together
at the last minute. A process is detailed which focuses on, in
turn, planning, situation analysis, identification of opportunities
and obstacles, development of goals and objectives, strategy
construction, and action plan development.

McConkey, Dale D. "How To Succeed and Fail with MBO." BUSINESS
QUARTERLY 37 (Winter 1972): 58-62.

Quick and organization-wide implementation is viewed as likely
to lead to failure. Outside consultant help should be employed
to assist staff members in developing for themselves their own
form of the approach. A chart rates three implementation procedures (one level at a time, one department only, all levels
at once) by their disadvantages and advantages: cost, time

requirements, match to different types of organizations and managements, and probability of success.

_____. MBO FOR NONPROFIT ORGANIZATIONS. New York: AMACOM, 1975. 223 p.

The author makes the case for MBO as a system in this easy-to-read compilation of prescription, anecdotes, problems, and case studies. He defines the system in terms of objectives, plans, managerial direction and action, control (monitoring), and feedback. He contrasts the effects of such implementation alternatives as one department only; one level at a time; and all levels at once. Cases describe MBO at the U.S. Public Health Service, the University of Wisconsin Management Institute, Hartford Hospital, the Lutheran Social Services of Wisconsin and Upper Michigan, and Canada's Department of Veterans Affairs.

_____. "The Position and Function of Budgets in an MBO System." BUSINESS QUARTERLY 39 (Spring 1974): 44-50.

The author urges that budgets be closely tied to MBO processes. For example, budgets should be approved on the basis of the objectives and plans which have been formulated, and should be evaluated and tested for realism bsaed upon previous performance. Traditional budgets are obsolete under MBO, and budgeting should primarily be viewed as the planned allocation of resources according to the manager's objectives. Budgets can be expected to perform motivational as well as control functions, and competition for resources should be emphasized.

_____. "20 Ways to Kill Management by Objectives." MANAGEMENT REVIEW 61 (October 1972): 4-13.

The author believes that it is managers, not the approach itself, who are the cause of failure. The MBO process can be torpedoed by "telling 'em their objectives" leaving out staff managers, delegating executive direction, creating paper mills, ignoring feedback, emphasizing techniques over substance, failing to provide rewards, and failing to blend objectives.

McDonald, Frederick J., and Forehand, Garlie A. "A Design for Accountability in Education." NEW YORK UNIVERSITY EDUCATION QUARTERLY 4 (Winter 1973): 7-16.

New York City's problem-solving accountability concept underlies a system which diagnoses inadequate educational progress and prescribes a plan for corrective action. Teaching competence is assessed in relation to expected outcomes, not on performance alone. Schools with comparable student performance are to be compared against one another, minimum standards are proposed, and a student development index is suggested to illustrate performance.

McGaghie, William C., and Menges, Robert J. "Goal Attainment Scaling in Psychological Education." GOAL ATTAINMENT REVIEW 2 (1975): 23-32.

> The authors' interest in psychological education (learning intended to foster interpersonal competence, encourage self-actualization, or increase self-control) led to the use of behavioral self-modification projects as an optional activity during the study of behavioral psychology in undergraduate educational psychology courses. A case study, involving increasing study behavior, is discussed in terms of recorded changes in behavior and goal attainment scales.

McGivney, Joseph H., and Krahl, George R. "Accountability and its Implications for Education." PLANNING AND CHANGING 4 (Summer 1973): 89-97.

> The article defines accountability as the assignment of responsibility to individuals to the extent that they hold commensurate degrees of authority. The authors trace potential problems in implementation which may confront superintendents, principals, and teachers. As a manager, and as part of a team being held responsible, the accountable teacher must be able to accurately diagnose learning problems displayed by individual students, develop appropriate behavioral objectives, prescribe the appropriate learning activities to overcome these individual learning problems, and evaluate the program while it is in progress to make any modifications necessary in the behavioral objectives themselves or adjust the learning activities to insure optimum progress of the student towards the objectives.

McGregor, Douglas. "An Uneasy Look at Performance Appraisal." HARVARD BUSINESS REVIEW 32 (September-October 1972): 133-38.

> This is the classic article in which the author notes that managers are uncomfortable at playing God. He proposes that employees develop their own short-term goals and evaluate their performance themselves. Performance review sessions then can concentrate on employee strengths.

Mackay, John A.H. "Management by Objective in the Canada Post Office." CANADIAN PERSONNEL 18 (January 1971): 13-17.

> The Canadian Deputy Postmaster General tells the Public Personnel Association how he will apply the MBO approach he had employed at I.T.T. within the post office. He feels that the personnel office will have an important role in implementation, because of its vested interest in job descriptions for classification purposes and objectivity in approaching organizational issues.

MacKenzie, R. Alec, and Varney, Glenn H. "The Missing Link in MBO." BUSINESS QUARTERLY 38 (Autumn 1973): 72-80.

The missing link involves the failure of companies to integrate MBO into their total schemes of management. The authors suggest application of the process throughout all management functions. Top management must become committed to MBO, and the process should be implemented from the top down, they argue. Line officers, not staff members, should have implementation responsibilities, and immediate results should not be expected.

Magoon, Albert J.; Martuza, Victor R.; and Fillos, Rita M. CRITIQUE OF THE DELAWARE EDUCATIONAL ASSESSMENT PROGRAM ACCOUNTABILITY MODEL. Newark: University of Delaware, n.d. 10 p.

The authors find that there is little consensus among either parents or teachers about what the accountability model should be doing, although more than nine of ten respondents would not in practice endorse its prescriptions for resource allocation. In particular, there is disagreement over the absence of absolute performance standards within the model.

Mahler, Walter R. "Management by Objectives: A Consultant's Viewpoint." TRAINING AND DEVELOPMENT JOURNAL 26 (April 1972): 16-19.

These consultant recommendations focus on achievement of organization-wide acceptance of the idea, and on obtaining the necessary behavior to allow the MBO program to be implemented successfully. MBO goals must be anchored to key managerial responsibilities. Types of goals include operating goals, relationship goals, and self-development or self-improvement goals.

Maiben, Dean H., and Schwabe, Charles J. "Management by Objectives." In LAST TANGO IN BOSTON, pp. 83-128. Washington, D.C.: National Training and Development Service, 1972.

This is an excellent case discussion of MBO implementation in the Village of Barrington, Illinois. The program was designed to fulfill organizational developmental and participatory management functions, but group problem solving failed to help office workers win acceptance of their demand for an end to Saturday morning village hall office hours. Public works employees, however, succeeded in getting a worn-out truck substantially repaired. After initial organization-wide efforts stalled, a second effort was directed at department heads. However, implementation was further slowed by the failure of computer software consultants to install a performance budgeting data system in a timely manner.

Malek, Frederick V. "Managing for Results in the Federal Government." BUSINESS HORIZONS 17 (April 1974): 23-28.

This key Nixon aide, responsible for implementation of the federal MBO system writes of the need to spotlight priorities, the difficulty in establishing accountability, and the problems of follow-through in a crisis-dominated environment. He and his colleagues looked for certain key features in each proposed objective: feasibility and achievability within budget constraints; importance to and consistency with presidential policies; extent of its measurability; and its potential for accomplishment.

_____. WASHINGTON'S HIDDEN TRAGEDY: THE FAILURE TO MAKE GOVERNMENT WORK. New York: Free Press, 1978. 292 p.

The author traces the difficulties a president faces in undertaking long-range planning, since "the analysis of where one is overwhelms the consideration of where one should be going," and lawyers and managers skilled at problem solving frequently lack enthusiasm for planning. He also details the history of the initial HEW MBO efforts and the subsequent government-wide implementation of the approach under Roy Ash, director of the Office of Management and Budget. He believes that key executive support is crucial, and that, at the outset, clear objectives must be enunciated and communicated to the organization as a whole. The system must work on a line manager-to-subordinate, not staff-to-staff basis. Objectives should be stated in terms of end results to be achieved and require simple plans or milestones with assigned responsibilities. Frequent follow-up meetings should be capped by a comprehensive end-of-year review.

Marik, Robert H., and McFee, Thomas S. "The Management Conference: Key to HEW's MBO System." BUREAUCRAT 2 (Winter 1974): 378-84.

The management conference is discussed as a mechanism which has helped HEW secretaries to run their department. For example, Elliot Richardson used it to "get a handle" on the department's work, and as a forum to communicate his ideas and concepts. Direct reporting to the secretary is viewed as helping to motivate managers, and the conferences are organized around problem-solving requirements.

Marimont, Rosalind B.; Maize, Kennedy P.; and Harley, Ernest. "Using FAIR to Set Numerical EEO Goals." PUBLIC PERSONNEL MANAGEMENT 5 (May-June 1976): 191-98.

"Goals" and "timetables" are the performance measures to which employers are committed in their affirmative action plans for equal employment opportunity hiring. FAIR (Feasible Allocation to Improve Representation) is a modification of the technique adopted in the consent decree settlement of the American Telephone and Telegraph suit. The technique relies heavily on the ethnic makeup of the applicant pool, and explicitly quantifies both the "advantage" for women and minority group members, and "limits" on the vacancies to be allocated to these groups, thereby protecting the interests of white males. By forthrightly and bluntly addressing so many basic questions of social philosophy, FAIR provides an excellent demonstration of the difficulty in defining performance measures.

Mason, Edward G., Jr. ASSESSING GOAL ATTAINMENT SCALING AS A PROGRAM EVALUATION APPROACH IN 25 TITLE I PROJECTS DURING FISCAL YEARS 1975 AND 1976. Madison: Wisconsin Division of Mental Hygiene, Program Evaluation and Research Section, 17 February 1977. 5 p.

Goal attainment scaling was employed to evaluate Title I ESEA projects, and this memorandum applies the A-VICTORY model in assessing its implementation. High staff turnover and resistance to multiple reporting requirements were major problems. In particular, participants resisted attempting to predict the time frames needed to achieve results, preferring to focus on short-term objectives.

_____. CLIENT-SPECIFIC PROGRAM EVALUATION: GOAL ATTAINMENT SCALING. Madison: Wisconsin Division of Mental Hygiene, Program Evaluation and Research Section, 1975. 36 p.

This is a manual to be used in the evaluation of Title I-funded day care projects. Users are warned that they should not be vague in defining outcome measures; that they should design scales which are both exhaustive and continuous; and that each of the five levels should be mutually exclusive. Examples are provided of such formats as initial status reports, follow-up guides, scoring procedures, and conversion tables to turn scores into percentile ranks.

Mauger, Paul; Stolberg, Arnold; Audette, Donna; and Simonini, Charles. "A Study of the Construct Validity of Goal Attainment Scaling." GOAL ATTAINMENT REVIEW 1 (1974): 13-19.

Discussion is presented about issues surrounding the face, content, and construct validity of the approach. A study is described which looked at twenty-eight Hennepin County Mental Health Service patients who completed Minnesota Multiphasic Personality Inventory follow-up tests. Findings support the construct validity of goal attainment scaling.

Meyer, Herbert H.; Kay, Emanuel; and French, John R.P., Jr. "Split Roles in Performance Appraisal." HARVARD BUSINESS REVIEW 43 (January-February 1965): 123-29.

These General Electric officials evaluate the effectiveness of their performance appraisal program. They find that more MBO-style procedures are preferrable: mutual goal setting instead of

criticism; reviews of performance without salary or promotion in
the balance; and day-by-day rather than once-a-year review.
Appraisal discussions previously revolved around salary-action
justifications and had little influence on future job performance.

Michigan. Department of Education. A STAFF RESPONSE TO THE REPORT:
AN ASSESSMENT OF THE MICHIGAN ACCOUNTABILITY SYSTEM. Lansing:
May 1974. 35 p.

This is the staff response to the bombshell dropped by House,
Rivers, and Stufflebeam (see p. 110). It finds the teachers-
funded study to include biases, contain inaccuracies, and rely
upon "somewhat unrigorous and hurriedly-gathered information."
Discussion focuses around such areas as the comprehensiveness
of the performance objectives, the process developed to select
these objectives, and the correctness of trying to determine objectives to be used throughout the state. The staff argues that
test data should be used for needs assessments, rather than as a
report card ranking or evaluating all of the state's schools.

Model Cities Evaluation Institute. BASIC CONCEPTS AND DEFINITIONS.
Module 2. Washington, D.C.: University Research Corp., 1970. 13 p.

This was a publication designed to help local model cities
agencies plan efforts directed toward improving the quality of
life in model neighborhoods. Program objectives state what is
to be accomplished in these terms, detailing within what time
frame and by how much but not how. Project objectives are
more limited by their designation of specific target groups. In-
put and output concepts are defined in their relationship to objectives.

Molander, C.F. "Management by Objectives in Perspective." JOURNAL OF
MANAGEMENT STUDIES 9 (February 1972): 74-81.

The author warns that when a basically collaborative technique
is used to bolster an authoritarian managerial structure, cooperation and commitment will not increase (and may be thwarted in
Great Britain by the growth of managerial trade unionism). Sub-
optimization may also result either by avoidance of high risk
programs, or by the selection of easily attained, easily quantified goals. To the author, MBO is always open to the dangers
of being punishment-centered, unless it is part of an overall
organizational development and participative management approach.

Monsanto Co. THE MANAGEMENT STYLE. Creve Coeur, Mo.: September
1974. 23 p.

This report helps to provide across the corporation "a common
management style and language, the purpose of which is to aid

in the development of an environment which will encourage our management people to maximize the development and use of their abilities for their own growth and satisfaction, and for their fullest contribution to the achievement of Monsanto's corporate objectives." This management style involves assigning responsibility by results and goals that best contribute to overall company objectives; a staff system whose primary role is to help the line to achieve results; and a decision-making system in which everyone is encouraged to make decisions which result in action.

Morrisey, George L. "Making MBO Work--The Missing Link." TRAINING AND DEVELOPMENT JOURNAL 39 (February 1976): 3-11.

> The author, another advocate of participative management, argues for the implementation of MBO, because it encourages the following: commitment rather than compliance; innovation balanced by reality; every manager to be president; negotiation and mutual agreement; a rational basis for review and feedback on progress toward objectives; a common language base; intergroup communication and teamwork; and a tangible rationale for budgeting and funding requests.

_____. "MBO Questions and Answers." PUBLIC PERSONNEL MANAGEMENT 5 (March-April 1976): 96-102.

> Problems with MBO are addressed from the following perspective: "MBO must be seen as working primarily for the individual manager using it and only secondarily to satisfy some organizational need." The article features such private sector exhortations as the need to "sell your customers, the legislators," without great deference to the distinctions between working within democratically and economically accountable systems.

_____. "Without Control, MBO is a Waste of Time." MANAGEMENT REVIEW 64 (February 1975): 11-17.

> The article contends that a mechanism has to be established to ensure that objectives which are set are, in fact, accomplished. Controlling, although a nonproducing activity (in fact, an inhibitor of production), is needed to make the red flag pop up when an organization is getting into trouble. Effective controlling provides for adequate visibility in a timely fashion with the least expenditure of time and effort.

Murphy, Jerome T., and Cohen, David K. "Accountability in Education-- The Michigan Experience." PUBLIC INTEREST 36 (Summer 1974): 53-81.

> This article is an excellent historical case study of Michigan's state accountability model. In particular, the writers compare the political acceptability of norm-referenced and objectives-

referenced testing, noting that the latter approach in fact re-
flects new professionally developed norms. They point out that
the earlier system reduced all of the available information to
a few statistics, which were often misleading, while the subsequent system produces an avalanche of data, not easily interpretable for framing decisions. Another study finding indicated
little correlation between low performance and limited resources,
torpedoing reform efforts. Also detailed is Michigan's attempted
Chapter 3 resource allocation program, tying resource allocation
to the attainment of performance goals. In reality, the state
chose to waive the imposition of this concept during each of
the first two years of the program's existence.

Newland, Chester. "MBO Concepts in the Federal Government." BUREAU-
CRAT 2 (Winter 1974): 351-61; 421-26.

MBO objectives should each convey to people generally what is
to be done; insure that responsible people know precisely what
they are to do within a given time; involve commitment of responsible people to accomplishment of expected results; and provide criteria for evaluating performance. Federal implementation involved a recognition of the need for both integration for
unity of purposes and central coordination, and for differentiated
processes suited to diverse agency situations. Common obstacles
may include the dilution of efforts among multiple goals, employee-
employer goal divergence, crisis management requirements, organizational structure constraints, and cost inflation and macro-
manpower problems. In the public sector additional statutes may
determine basic goals and objectives, organizational structure
and processes, and pay and other economic rewards.

_____. "Policy/Program Objectives and Federal Management: The Search for
Government Effectiveness." PUBLIC ADMINISTRATION REVIEW 36 (January-
February 1976): 20-27.

The author tells the story of how Roy Ash approached the Office
of Management and Budget with the belief that budgeting was
only one of a series of related management processes, which
would ideally flow from a continuous process of program analysis
tuned to established objectives and achieved results. However,
after he declined to prescribe what form the process should take,
the federal agencies' responses varied greatly in quality. OMB
then developed instructions requiring the submission of objectives
alongside budget requests. This article relates the MBO efforts
to other federal initiatives in the areas of reorganization, social
indicators, productivity, and program evaluation.

_____, ed. MBO AND PRODUCTIVITY BARGAINING IN THE PUBLIC SECTOR.
Chicago: International Personnel Management Association, 1974. 80 p.

The editor believes that MBO provides a method for pursuing

fundamental governmental responsibilities: setting objectives, evaluating progress, and evaluating results. He feels that the greatest problem with the approach is the determination of "whose objectives are authoritative." An article by Elsa Porter discusses MBO as the best approach for managing personnel functions directed toward enhancing productivity.

New York City. Mayor's Management Advisory Board. MANAGEMENT PLAN AND REPORT MANUAL. New York: May 1976.

> The management plan is designed to assist in review and evaluation of each city agency's management performance, and to identify emerging problems and the initiation of appropriate corrective action. This manual details how to define a mission statement; present performance indicators and operating statistics; ascertain priority according to three citywide (top-down) criteria for priority; and explain variances.

_____. MANAGEMENT PLAN FOR THE DEPARTMENT OF PARKS AND RECREATION FOR THE FISCAL YEAR 1977. New York: 28 June 1976. 62 p.

> This is a good example of the agency response to the MBO planning system set up by Jack Ukeles during the Beame administration. A discussion of the agency's missions is followed by the ranking of its priorities consistent with citywide priorities. Performance reports are submitted in voluminous detail, preparatory to eventual summarization in the mayor's report to the public. In a link to the issue analysis process, an agenda of agency issues is listed, subject to subsequent analysis.

_____. THE MAYOR'S MANAGEMENT REPORT. New York: 18 February 1977. 152 p.

> The first plan introduces the three mayoral priorities, which provide the strategic organizing principle for the report: protection of life, preservation and development of the economy, and neighborhood development. Agency reports generally respond to these directions with discussion of their relevant activities and tabulations of their performance.
>
> 19 August 1977 (Supplemental): 120 p. In this second report, measures of service response are included, when possible, including backlog data, and quality indicators are sometimes included (e.g., Project Scorecard Sanitation ratings).
>
> 20 February 1978: 109 p. This is the first report of a new mayor, issued during his second month in office. Mayoral "priorities" are procedural, rather than substantive: work force reduction, absorption of inflationary price increases, welfare fraud reduction, and improved revenue generation. There is, however, a statement supporting preservation of essential services, and key programs to improve the economy and aid in job de-

velopment. The previous strategic direction of MBO planning through priority assessment seems however to have been lost or minimized in the shuffle and turnover of strategy developers.

_____. PERFORMANCE PLAN (MBO-NYC). New York: January-June 30, 1976. 13 p.

This is a brief summary document which lays out the overhead agency-operating agency MBO contract, and explicates mayoral priorities. Criteria-choice matrixes for determining the priorities of objectives are followed by agency "performance standards and targets" report forms. There is also discussion of and forms for the designation of agency improvement projects.

_____. PROGRAM STATEMENT (MBO-NYC). New York: 15 December 1975. 11 p.

This paper is the basic written document in the New York Management Plan effort. It notes the requirements of the city's financial plan for effective management, the opportunity presented by the financial crisis to attempt to implement lasting management improvements, and the agreement of management and labor to take action to do so. MBO-NYC is the process proposed to act upon these commitments. Key conditions which are detailed include the absence of a single measure of performance, such as profitability; the application of top-down mayoral priorities; identification of critical issues; new mayoral policy review procedures; gradual phase-in; and experimentation with new incentives.

Niedermeyer, Fred, and Klein, Stephen. "An Empirical Evaluation of a District Teachers' Accountability Program." PHI DELTA KAPPAN 53 (October 1972): 100-104.

The Newport-Mesa Unified School District in California developed the Staff Performance Improvement and Appraisal Plan. During appraisal cycles, teachers submit instructional objectives in two subject areas, and principals evaluate student performance in regard to these objectives. During improvement cycles, teachers submit lesson plans to teams of colleagues who observe and evaluate performance.

Norton, Steven D. "Management by Results in the Public Sector." PUBLIC PRODUCTIVITY REVIEW 2 (Fall 1976): 20-33.

The author believes that the two approaches should be distinguished because classic MBO is inappropriate in the public sector. He feels that the private sector has more management continuity, and industrial democracy measures are inapplicable in the public sector (it is the influence of the voters which should be broadened within a democracy). Management by results involves far less autonomous behavior on the part of junior levels of management.

O'Connell, Gerald. TEAM POLICING PROGRAM. St. Louis, Mo.: St. Louis, Metropolitan Police Department, Planning and Development Division, 17 December 1976. 36 p.

Both the Dayton and St. Louis team policing programs have emphasized decentralized objectives-setting. This is the six-months evaluation of the St. Louis project. It details both the objectives and priorities established for the district to be policed in this manner, and describes the work responsibilities of each of the participants in the team policing process.

Odiorne, George S. "MBO in State Government." PUBLIC ADMINISTRATION REVIEW 36 (January-February 1976): 28-33.

A case study indicates that superiors lacked a clear view of what was expected of line managers; governmental functions were sometimes hard to spell out in performance terms; and performance measures were frequently hard to determine. The author suggests two sets of objectives: (1) a long-range set prior to budgeting and (2) a short-range set after budgeting. He also notes that resource allocation decisions associated with MBO are likely to be influenced by the requirements of managers for resources needed to bring off their commitments.

_____. "The Politics of Implementing MBO." BUSINESS HORIZONS 17 (June 1974): 13-21.

Three approaches to overcoming political resistance are described by this expert: authoritarian directives, persuasion, and educational programs. The power structure's interests must be assessed, since MBO has the capacity to shift the locus of power. The author also suggests that those who implement MBO examine unit loyalties; the reactions of individualists; status symbols; organizational form; and the effects of inter-unit alliances.

O'Reilly, Robert P., and Gorth, William P. "Alternatives to Accountability: Stool Pigeon vs. Servant and Soulmate." PLANNING AND CHANGING 3 (April 1972): 13-24.

The authors feel that the external development of performance objectives will lead to great staff anxieties, that public reporting may erode any remaining local confidence in the schools, and that the development of staff professionalism will be hindered by externally imposed changes. They wonder about the quality of the outcome measures proposed for use in accountability applications. Some levels of objectives described are terminal, approximations to terminal, course, and enabling objectives. Providing the general public with data comparing schools and programs is discouraged.

Ornstein, Allan C., ed. ACCOUNTABILITY FOR TEACHERS AND SCHOOL ADMINISTRATORS. Belmont, Calif.: Fearon Publishers, 1973. 135 p.

> This anthology, expanding upon Ornstein's article in NATION'S SCHOOLS (see below), includes selections ranging from Leon Lessinger's piece conceptualizing accountability (at least, movement from input- to output-oriented thinking in education), to articles placing the teacher's role into perspective, to accountability system design discussions by Henry Dyer, Steven Barro, and Felix Lopez.

_____. "Teacher Accountability." NATION'S SCHOOLS 89 (May 1972): 45-68.

> This collection begins with Robert Havighurst urging that accountability should be "joint," and not forced solely upon teachers. AFT President David Selden defines accountability as knee-jerk productivity ideology ("Accountability advocates approach education with all of the insight of an irate viewer fixing a television set. Give it a kick and see what happens.") Scott Thomson points out that, unlike other professionals, teachers cannot enforce the implementation of their prescriptions; students can't be forced to study and learn in recommended ways. W. James Popham advocates the use of teaching performance tests. Mario Fantini proposes new parent-teacher relationships as the basis for a reform approach to accountability. Henry Dyer describes the accountable teacher as a social experimenter testing out action alternatives and implementing the most promising. Hulda Grobman expresses concern that, if comparable teaching inputs result in differential outputs depending on environmental variables beyond teachers' control, and, if these outputs cannot be accurately predicted at our present state of knowledge, accountability may sacrifice long-term, more important outcomes for short-term, readily observable gains.

Ornstein, Allan C., and Talmage, Harriet. "The Rhetoric and the Realities of Accountability." TODAY'S EDUCATION 62 (September-October 1973): 70-80.

> The writers note that there are great problems in relying upon tests, evaluating student performance, as a basis for an accountability system. For example, Benjamin Bloom's seminal environmental research argues that children's general intelligence is 50 percent developed by age four and 80 percent developed by age eight. Further, there are unresolved debates over the variations in the pace of student learning development. Criterion-referenced, as opposed to norm-referenced, tests are more appropriate for accountability measurement systems, but are only in an early stage of design.

Orr, Dorothy. GUIDELINES FOR AFFIRMATIVE ACTION IN THE BANKING INDUSTRY. New York: New York State, Division of Human Rights, Bureau of Program Planning and Affirmative Action, 1972. 25 p.

These guidelines reflect the consensus of representatives of leading New York metropolitan-area commercial banks. Specific goals for hiring are proposed for each of the next five years. Statements of goals are also listed in the areas of recruitment, selection, promotion, executive training, and supportive programs. Other guidelines are proposed for affirmative action lending.

_____. GUIDELINES FOR AFFIRMATIVE ACTION IN THE INSURANCE INDUSTRY. New York: New York State, Division of Human Rights, Bureau of Program Planning and Affirmative Action, 1972. 25 p.

This set of guidelines is developed in a manner similar to the state document on banking. Goals and timetables for action within the state are agreed upon by eight of the major national life insurance companies.

Paine, Whiton Stewart. THE UTILITY OF GOAL ATTAINMENT SCALING FOR EDUCATIONAL EVALUATION. Research and Evaluation report 5. Chester, Pa.: Crozer-Chester Community Mental Health Center, Research and Evaluation Service, 1977. 24 p.

After explaining the approach, the author recounts goal attainment scaling experiences in the field of education--the work done by Gillis and Paine; by Hegion, Fish, and Grace; and by Gary H. Miller, all with children. He indicates that the approach is most useful in stable organizational environments, and may not be useful in many short-term projects or in programs undergoing rapid change. "Success" concepts may become confused with inappropriate expectations. It also may be difficult to compare performance across programs, since process, short-term, and long-term goals may be mixed together in the same outcome analysis. A study found that while therapists and interviewers similarly emphasized the twenty most common generic goal areas, they frequently differed markedly on the use of the different goals with individual clients.

Patton, Michael Quinn. UTILIZATION-FOCUSED EVALUATION. Beverly Hills, Calif.: Sage Publications, 1978. 303 p.

The author describes program administrators' goals clarification shuffle, executed either before or after presentation of evaluation findings. "Conflict configurations" may emerge when staffs are interviewed in order to ascertain their goals. There are discussions of multi-attribute utility measurement, the decision theoretic approach, and Michael Scriven's proposals for goal-free evaluation, which the author feels substitutes evaluators' goals for program staffs' goals. A case study on the Hill-Burton health facilities construction program illustrates the difficulty of defining performance criteria. See particularly chapters 6-7.

Peart, Leo F. "Management by Objectives." POLICE CHIEF 38 (April 1971):
54-56.

> Palo Alto's police research and training coordinator discusses
> that city's team policing program. Lieutenants and sergeants,
> for instance, are now called managers and supervisors, and case
> responsibility is placed upon the originating officer. Emphasis
> is placed upon the work to be done, rather than upon the bu-
> reaucratic relationships of "who is responsible to whom," and
> dealing with specific situations replaces emphasis on command
> relationships, as program goals become the principle focus of
> operations.

Peretz, Martin, ed. "Meritocracy and Its Discontents." NEW REPUBLIC, 15
October 1977, pp. 5-9; 12-26.

> This is a compendium of attacks on implementation of affirmative
> action programs. It was drafted in expectation of the Bakke
> decision, and includes articles ranging from Seymour Martin
> Lipset and William Schneider's review of public opinion polls
> ("an emerging national consensus"); to Leonard Fein's article
> on Jewish community attitudes ("Merit is inscribed in the DNA
> that Jews carry and transmit"); to Eliot Marshall's warnings of
> racial certifications to come; to an attack upon male-female
> touch football team rules, indicating that the "goals and time-
> tables" in the rules somehow dishonor proper playing of the game.

Perrow, Charles. "The Analysis of Goals in Complex Organizations." AMERI-
CAN SOCIOLOGICAL REVIEW 26 (December 1961): 854-66.

> In this key sociological contribution to the literature, the author
> focuses on the goals embedded in major operating policies and
> the daily decisions of personnel, and how these goals are shaped
> by the organization's problems and tasks, since these tasks de-
> termine the characteristics of those who will dominate the or-
> ganization. The author feels that there are four basic organi-
> zational tasks: securing capitalization; winning acceptance in
> the form of basic legitimization of activity; the marshalling of
> necessary skills; and internal and external coordination of staff,
> clients, and consumers. Voluntary general hospitals are ex-
> amined to develop this perspective.

Pfeffer, Leo. "Quotas, Compensation, and Open Enrollment." CONGRESS
BI-WEEKLY (American Jewish Congress) 39 (25 February 1972): 4-9.

> This is a good, clear, simple discussion of the basic pros and
> cons of the issue, focusing on the use of quotas to assure that
> promises of integration and nondiscrimination are being kept.
> Establishing a minimal level of compliance protexts against to-
> kenism. "Aside from compensation for past wrongs, preferential
> treatment by law is justifiable when it serves to achieve an end

deemed beneficial to the community." The author also points out the argument that, in the absence of affirmative action, it may be impossible to overcome discrimination in the society to achieve racial justice.

Pollak, Richard. "Reporters' Report Cards." MORE 6 (September 1976): 30-32.

The author describes the performance appraisal system initiated by the NEW YORK TIMES. Seven categories of performance are evaluated: accuracy; lucid, grammatical, and intelligent writing; writing under deadline pressure; news sense; quantity; initiative and perseverance; and reporting techniques. The Newspaper Guild tried to halt imposition of the system by asking the National Labor Relations Board to classify it as a bargainable issue. They declined to do so.

Popham, W. James. "California's Precedent-Setting Teacher Evaluation Law." EDUCATIONAL RESEARCHER 1 (July 1972): 13-15.

The California legislature passed the Stull Bill which requires teacher performance appraisal, based upon established standards and techniques for assessing student progress in each area of study and assessment of teacher competence as it relates to the established standards. Teacher competence must then be partially assessed in terms of pupil growth.

Prettyman, Julia. CITY LAYOFFS: THE EFFECT ON MINORITIES AND WOMEN. New York: City Commission on Human Rights, Government Employment Unit, April 1976. 29 p.

This report describes the recommendations made by the commission to mitigate the adverse impact of retrenchment upon minorities and women. During the financial crisis, for example, 51.2 percent of Hispanic workers and 35 percent of black employees lost their jobs. City guidelines preclude layoffs which are not job-related and not dictated by business necessity. Separations are to be analyzed as to whether they perpetuate the effect of past discrimination.

Raia, Anthony. "Goal-Setting and Self-Control." JOURNAL OF MANAGEMENT STUDIES 2 (February 1965): 34-53.

To the author, MBO should encourage the proper integration of economic purpose and personal goals, through the active participation of the subordinate in establishing tangible work goals and exercising self-control over activities designed to achieve those goals. The "goals and controls" system at Purex takes managers away from daily operations considerations in order to plan the use of resources; helps to pinpoint problem areas; and allows for the objective appraisal of individual performance.

Ricks, Frances A., and Weinstein, Malcolm S. HOME-CARE EFFECTIVENESS MEASURES FOR 1975-76. Downsview, Ont.: Dellcrest Children's Centre Research Department, 1976. 7 p.

> This report measures the effectiveness of home care direct services, in order to ascertain whether the agency is better at dealing with some goals than others and at working with some clients than with others. Goals are set in three areas: social skills, self-image, and feelings.

_____. "The Influence of Modified Goal Attainment Scaling Procedures on Treatment Outcome." GOAL ATTAINMENT REVIEW 2 (1975): 65-70.

> The authors compared these methods with broader measures of treatment outcome, and treatment outcomes for clients whose therapists did and did not employ modified goal attainment scaling. They find that the approach's greatest use is in measuring the change on treatment objectives as seen by the clinician, but that its value as a treatment outcome measurement system remains unproven.

Riesing, Thomas F., and Peele, Stanton. U.S. DEPARTMENT OF HEALTH, EDUCATION, AND WELFARE (A) AND (B). Boston: Intercollegiate Case Clearing House, 1972. Case (A) 9-172-284: 29 p.; case (B) 9-172-285: 24 p.

> These two cases are an invaluable teaching aid for instruction in MBO. They illustrate the difficulties of winning line manager acceptance of a concept which may benefit them in their work, as well as appraise their performance. The cases might best be used in conjunction with other readings on HEW case conferences and the difficulties of defining performance measures, particularly for programs on agency funds, but does not administer operationally. Implementation efforts for the HEW Operational Planning System are described at the Food and Drug Administration, the Office of Education, and the Health Services and the Mental Health Administration.

Riggs, Robert O. "Management by Objectives: Its Utilization in the Management of Administrative Performance." CONTEMPORARY EDUCATION 43 (January 1972): 129-33.

> The director of educational development and research at the University of Tennessee proposes an MBO approach in which each professional employee annually defines his or her objectives, subject to performance review, which would influence salary and tenure decisions. Administrative performance criteria might include: awareness and anticipation; initiative; sense of responsibility; commitment to excellence; commitment to service; participation in campus community activities; responsiveness; and communications skills.

Rose, Richard. "Implementation and Evaporation: The Record of MBO." PUBLIC ADMINISTRATION REVIEW 37 (January-February 1977): 64-71.

> The author writes that MBO in the federal government exchanged the difficulties of coping with immediate management problems for the difficulties of implementing intended solutions. He argues that in the long run, this is not problem solving and that the Nixon administration attempted to shift attention from problems of choice to problems of management. MBO, when implemented, was undermined by the cancellation of management review conferences, and the preference expressed for fire fighting. Too much of the effort was explicitly managerially oriented and apolitical, and OMB largely lost interest.

_____. MANAGING PRESIDENTIAL OBJECTIVES. New York: Free Press, 1974. 180 p.

> In this first major book-length exploratory study of MBO in the Nixon administration, the author notes the largely inactive role of the chief executive in the process and the limitations upon the capacity of executive agencies to evaluate performance. Particularly interesting is the description of the objectives-setting process, as it was played out in different agencies. He discusses the approach in terms of administration criteria for its success: improved communications; the fostering of problem spotting; and improved accountability of managers to supervisors. He argues that the most important questions will be monitored by the political process (those involving the roles of government). Since MBO in the administration was not concerned about choices between alternatives, it was largely outside this political process.

Ross, Harry S.; Maull, Perry J.; and Smerk, George M. MANAGEMENT BY OBJECTIVES APPLIED TO TRANSPORTATION SYSTEM MANAGEMENT. Presented at the Conference on Transportation System Management, November 1976, Minneapolis, conducted by the Transportation Research Board. Washington, D.C.: U.S. Transportation Research Board, 1976. 6 p.

> The authors are preoccupied with the problem of the comparative lack of performance accountability on the part of public transit systems. Once measurable goals and objectives are defined, it will be possible to develop a truly well-thought-out action plan to attain them. For example, effective media liaison might have relieved some of the difficulties encountered in opening up the Santa Monica Freeway diamond lane.

Routh, Frederick B., and Waldo, Everett A., eds. AFFIRMATIVE ACTION IN EMPLOYMENT IN HIGHER EDUCATION. Proceedings of a consultation held in Washington 9 and 10 September 1975. Washington, D.C.: U.S. Commission on Civil Rights, 1976. 239 p.

> Revised Order 4 (and its goals and timetables) is a featured

topic, particularly in the papers of James Henry and Howard Glickstein. The Richard Lester and Carnegie Council studies of this issue are an important basis for discussion at the consultation, in which federal regulations, HEW guidelines and practices, and university reactions are all explored in detail. Opponents of the approach, such as Miro Todorovich and Thomas Sowell, also present their arguments.

Salasin, John, and Entingh, Daniel J. AN APPROACH TO IDENTIFYING OBJECTIVES FOR TARGETED RESEARCH PROGRAMS. Washington, D.C.: MITRE Corp., METREK Division, March 1977. 50 p.

A five-step approach is detailed. Step 1 specifies scope by stating the mission, describing the context and intellectual resources, and identifying constraints. Step 2 defines targets, which refine the mission statement, and step 3 requires a look at the roles which objectives may play (program planning, project selection, administrative support, evaluation of project and program progress, and diffusion and utilization of findings). Step 4 lays out a structure fixing the relationship between targets and objectives, some of which should be measurable. The final step involves a process for collecting information necessary to identify potential objectives. This procedure has been used to identify potential children's mental health services research objectives.

Santa-Barbara, Jack; Woodward, Christel A.; Levin, Sol; Goodman, John T.; Streiner, David L.; Muzzin, Linda; and Epstein, Nathan B. "Variables Related to Outcome in Family Therapy: Some Preliminary Analysis." GOAL ATTAINMENT REVIEW 1 (1974): 5-12.

The study examines family therapy cases in which a six to twelve-year-old child from an intact family is the client, as a result of academic or behavioral school problems. Goal attainment does not correlate significantly with client satisfaction or recidivism in the findings.

Schuster, Frederick E. "An Evaluation of the Management by Objectives Approach to Performance Appraisal." Ph.D. dissertation, Harvard, Graduate School of Business Administration, 1 December 1968. 423 p.

This study attempted to measure the extent to which MBO had been adopted by companies, and the level of its success in application. The author finds that 70 percent of the Fortune 500 companies surveyed conduct performance appraisals, and 35 percent of these companies apply MBO. Employee motivation and employee training and development are the principle reasons for its use. When viewed as a personnel program, it meets with resistance and has little effect; while, when used as a new approach to management, it may have a significant positive influence on motivation, commitment, and morale (and less frequently, on productivity and profitability.) Implementation is usually not uniformly successful throughout a company; even the most successful processes continue to confront some recalcitrant managers. Top management commitment is the most important requirement for success.

Schwartz, Alfred I., and Clarren, Sumner N. THE CINCINNATI TEAM PO-LICING EXPERIMENT: A SUMMARY REPORT. Washington, D.C.: Police Foundation, 1977. 63 p.

This team policing program asked patrol officers and specialists to participate actively in team problem solving and decision making, and to help set goals. However, in application, MBO was found to be used by headquarters to impose standardized demands for increasingly rigid levels of measurable activity. Officers' MBO plans were continually returned, until head-quarters priorities were included. Headquarters used the approach to recentralize control and destroy the autonomy of the teams. A sergeant claimed that "M.B.O. is the biggest para-site of all--it sucks the life blood of the department. It will cripple the supervision and eventually no one will have time for anything."

Scott, Dru. "Productive Partnerships--Coupling MBO and TA." MANAGEMENT REVIEW 65 (November 1976): 12-19.

Transactional analysis is proposed as the technique to assist in developing the personal relationships needed to implement MBO since, according to the author, the person who does not express wants promptly and directly wastes both time and energy. MBO, she feels, works best when accomplishing objectives not only makes sense but feels good now.

Shain, Martin. PREREQUISITES FOR EVALUATIVE RESEARCH IN HALFWAY HOUSES--DECISIONMAKING AIDS FOR ADMINISTRATOR AND RESEARCHER. Substudy no. 683. Toronto: Addiction Research Foundation, 1975. 18 p.

Halfway house evaluations have frequently been negative, be-cause they have been conducted prematurely--before the agencies have stated goals; before the available means for achieving these goals are consistent; and before the programs appropriately relate to the needs of the population served. An example of the ques-tions which need to be asked of a halfway house is presented: how the client population and conceptions of their potential for change are defined; how client nonconformity is dealt with; how goals are defined; how decisions are made; what the staff believes in; and how staff and residents see themselves and their roles.

_____. THE SMALL RESIDENTIAL CARE CENTRE AS AN ORGANIZATION. Project D-234. Toronto: Addiction Research Foundation, 1971. 35 p.

> The author discusses residential care centers as organizations, and lays out his model of goal consistency: a clear statement of internally consistent goals, endorsed by the staff; appropriately relating to the needs of those it serves; a decision-making process consistent with goals; values and behavioral capacities of staff which are consistent with goals; and goals consistent with the demands of the surrounding community.

_____. TOWARD A GENERAL FRAMEWORK FOR EVALUATING INTERVEN- TION IN CERTAIN LARGE ORGANIZATIONS. Substudy no. 536. Toronto: Addiction Research Foundation, 1973. 37 p.

> The author contrasts the relationships among goals, task struc- tures, and social structures in three different areas: education, corrections, and industry.

Shanahan, Donald T. PATROL ADMINISTRATION: MANAGEMENT BY OB- JECTIVES. Boston: Holbrook Press, 1975. 550 p.

> This is a basic text addressing fundamental police patrol ques- tions such as command and control; reporting, records, and in- formation; manpower distribution; weapons; special operations; and team policing. A chapter on "patrol planning" details ap- plications of management by objectives in areas such as preven- tion, criminal apprehension, and support (examples of outputs and inputs are specified).

Shebuski, Donald. "An Accountability System Verifying Task Accomplishments for Organizational Leaders." Ph.D. dissertation, University of Wisconsin, 1971. 332 p.

> This study examines specific performance measures as possible evidence for the evaluation of the work of a superintendent of schools. The author found a high degree of homogeneity among school board members in their attitudes toward accountability measures, but that conflicts in perspective between board mem- bers and superintendents were especially pronounced in larger districts.

Sherwin, Douglas S. "Management of Objectives." HARVARD BUSINESS RE- VIEW 54 (May-June 1976): 149-60.

> The MBO approach implemented at Phillips Products Company recognizes that an organization, in achieving its objectives, requires coordinated activity beyond the successful performance of individual tasks. The author notes that the failure to organ- ize to meet strategic organization-wide objectives is a frequent problem with MBO in operation. He believes that project man-

agement efforts prove uncompetitive in obtaining time, power, and resources; and proposes an "objectives grid" approach, in which teams are accountable for implementing objectives which receive priority (those which can be secured with available resources).

Sherwood, Frank P., and Page, William J., Jr. "MBO and Public Management." PUBLIC ADMINISTRATION REVIEW 36 (January-February 1976): 5-12.

> The authors discuss MBO as a managerial tactic, rather than as a system. In regard to HEW, they indicate that OPS (Operational Planning System) was valuable as an informational tracking system and as a formal review process, rather than as a basis for an allocation strategy. They evaluate the familiar private-public sector analogy, and point out, in regard to implementing MBO in the public sector, that: (1) work frequently is allocated to the public sector, because lack of knowledge or uncertainty make it infeasible or too risky for the private sector; (2) stated objectives may not be real objectives; and (3) there are no commonly accepted standards for monitoring performance or measuring the achievement of many public sector objectives.

Shetty, Yermal Krishna, and Carlisle, Howard M. "A Study of Management by Objectives in a Professional Organization." JOURNAL OF MANAGEMENT STUDIES 12 (February 1975): 1-11.

> This article studies MBO for a year at a public university of nine thousand students, with six hundred faculty members. The findings indicate that strong organizational support was significantly related to success (e.g., in departments which had devoted substantial effort to defining goals and priorities). Participants who felt more highly involved also perceived that the program yielded better results. Goal characteristics correlated with the program's success included clarity and specificity; compatability of departmental and personal goals; and action orientation.

Singular, Stephen. "Has MBO Failed?" MBA 9 (October 1975): 47-50.

> This popular magazine article notes that researchers have found that less than half of the Fortune 500 companies use the approach, only 10 percent find it to be a success, and only 2 percent feel that it is highly successful. Complaints are rehashed about difficulties in setting arbitrary goals dependent for their success upon external forces, and the tendency to set too low, easily attainable goals. Measurement can often be a private sector problem, as well as a public sector problem, and frequently companies are unwilling to take all the time needed for successful implementation.

Spaner, Steven D. ANALYSIS OF THE SITE ANALYSIS STUDY. St. Louis, Mo.: Citizens Education Task Force, June 1977. 83 p.

> Site management is a current concept of decentralized management in public school districts, in which superintendents and principals administer responsibility centers, and comparative performance is evaluated. This study is a compilation of responses by current administrators to a questionnaire surveying their views on this matter. For example, senior administrators desire more budget preparation influence and greater year-round budget control.

Spano, Robert M., and Lund, Sander H. MANAGEMENT BY OBJECTIVES IN A HOSPITAL-BASED SOCIAL SERVICE UNIT. Minneapolis, Minn.: Program Evaluation Resource Center, Phase 1, December 1973: 21 p.; phase 2, January 1975: 26 p.

> These two reports offer a brief but simple and clear case study. Objectives setting, they find, helps in communications with other agencies by being explicitly accountable; assists in rationalizing administration; and leads to increases in staff efficiency.

Strauss, George. MBO: A CRITICAL VIEW. Reprint no. 359. Berkeley: University of California, Institute of Industrial Relations, 1972. 5 p.

> The author feels that there is a great deal of conflict over what the purpose of MBO should be--management control, participating management, or methodology for decision making. He feels that the requirements for developing a common plan considerably limit the latitude available to individuals in setting their own goals. Even measurable standards sometimes help employees to "look good," rather than "be good." He warns that the most serious problems result in organizations where there is an incongruity between verbalized and actual levels of subordinate influence.

Swanstrom, William J., and Hedberg, Larry. "Broadening the Use of Goal Attainment Scaling in Residential Treatment--Moving Toward a More Complete Program Evaluation Design." GOAL ATTAINMENT REVIEW 1 (1974): 49-54.

> The Bethany Lutheran Home for Children is a residential treatment center for about forty-two socially vulnerable adolescents who are experiencing moderate to severe adjustment problems. Goal attainment scaling is used to identify clients making poor progress, before they are too far into the treatment program. Grouped results focus on individual, group, team, and program progress; post-treatment follow-up results; and the change process.

Tarter, Jim L. MANAGEMENT BY OBJECTIVES FOR PUBLIC ADMINISTRATORS. Washington, D.C.: National Training and Development Service, 1974. 13 p.

This is actually a six-page questions-and-answers introduction to the outlines for a series of three training modules. The modules' agendas are also outlined.

Thompson, James D., and McEwen, William J. "Organizational Goals and Environment: Goal-Setting As an Interaction Process." AMERICAN SOCIO-LOGICAL REVIEW 23 (February 1958): 23-31.

Goal setting is viewed not as a static element, but as a neces-sary and recurring problem facing any organization. The pro-cess is purposive but not necessarily rational, since the problem is essentially one of determining the relationship of the organi-zation to the larger society, which, in turn, becomes a ques-tion of what the society (or elements within it) wants done or can be persuaded to support.

Tosi, Henry L., and Carroll, Stephen. "Some Factors Affecting the Success of 'Management by Objectives.'" JOURNAL OF MANAGEMENT STUDIES 7 (May 1970): 209-23.

A survey involving 128 managers from a large manufacturer brings the authors to the conclusion that goal setting must be tailored by the manager to the different characteristics of in-dividual subordinates in order to minimize some negative con-sequences. For example, employees who need certainty, or who are unsure of their environment, relate better to their bosses, when the latter implement MBO. Those highly inter-ested in their job respond positively, as opposed to those who view MBO as threatening to the status quo.

Ukeles, Jacob B. REMARKS TO THE CITY CLUB OF NEW YORK. New York: New York City, Mayor's Management Advisory Board, 8 October 1976. 8 p.

In describing the management plan he developed to integrate strategic planning and priority setting with an MBO approach, the agency's former executive director compares requirements for planned management against the crisis-responsive nature of city government. He also discusses performance in terms of the public need to know how well government is doing, and con-temporary development of a focus on individual accountability. He urges that strategic questions (e.g., reevaluation of func-tions) be highlighted in management-planning efforts.

U.S. Civil Service Commission. Bureau of Intergovernmental Personnel Programs. GOALS AND TIMETABLES FOR EFFECTIVE AFFIRMATIVE ACTION. Washington, D.C.: Government Printing Office, 1973. 12 p.

This manual is designed for use by state and local governments, and it clearly lays out the MBO goals and timetables notions: work force analysis (internally and within the recruitment area), followed by estimation of employment opportunities opening up; the applicant flow; and setting of long-range versus short-range goals. An illustrative chart shows how to keep score.

Viteritti, Joseph P. "New York's Management Plan and Reporting System: A Descriptive Analysis." PUBLIC ADMINISTRATION REVIEW 38 (July-August 1978): 376-81.

This article describes the history and component parts of that city's management performance plan. The assignment of re-porting responsibilities within agencies away from line managers and to policy analysts, led in 1977 to an effort to further sharpen the department head-unit manager level of reporting within the plan network. The article fails to touch upon stra-tegic and resource allocation concepts in the plan.

Wallace, Robert T. "A New Test for Management by Objectives." BUREAU-CRAT 2 (Winter 1974): 362-67.

The author feels that federal MBO implementation efforts re-flected the view that a sound management philosophy is more important than an impressive management information system. The president's initiation of the program highlighted especially critical, high-priority items; established a results-oriented en-vironment; and encouraged managers to think through the actions needed to bring about results. At the time the article was written, the author, a staff person at the Office of Management and Budget felt follow-up would be needed in areas such as helping agencies to actually achieve results, developing new objectives, measurement, budgeting linkages, more comprehen-sive use, coordination, and decentralization.

Weed, Lawrence L. MEDICAL RECORDS, MEDICAL EDUCATION, AND PA-TIENT CARE. Cleveland, Ohio: Press of Case Western Reserve University, 1969. 250 p.

A basic text by the father of the problem-oriented medical record movement, this is an approach featuring a rationalized process in which treatment objectives flow naturally from diag-nostic assessment.

Weiss, Edmond. "Educational Accountability and the Presumption of Guilt." PLANNING AND CHANGING 3 (Fall 1972): 24-28.

Teachers feel that evaluation studies are designed to find fault with programs, that performance appraisal will be used to em-barrass or discredit them, and that performance contracting will result in unfair, invidious comparisons. Rational analysis does lead to rejection of all but the preferred alternative, and ac-countability--given the insulation educators previously have had from the public--carries a "palpable presumption of guilt."

Educators are urged to participate quite watchfully and carefully in the development of accountability models.

White, Buffy. GOAL ATTAINMENT SCALING IN REHABILITATION. No. 5. Chicago: Jewish Vocational Service Research Utilization Laboratory, September 1976. 52 p. Appendix.

This manual not only explains the approach, but also provides the forms and case studies needed in order to learn to apply the approach. A technical appendix describes pilot studies undertaken at two sites--Hibbing, Minnesota, and Madison, Wisconsin. These studies convinced this agency to advocate the use of the approach in rehabilitation agencies throughout the country.

Wickens, J.D. "Management by Objectives: An Appraisal." JOURNAL OF MANAGEMENT STUDIES 5 (October 1968): 365-79.

The author discusses MBO within the context of relevant organizational and human relationist theory, and details a case study of a British manufacturing plant with 3,500 workers. Improvements in efficiency were attributable to the development of an effective planning mechanism; the focus on key results areas; the impetus to respond more flexibly to environmental changes; the enhanced provision of information that managers need to make wise decisions; and the expansion of participation in the decision-making processes.

Wildavsky, Aaron. "The Strategic Retreat on Objectives." POLICY ANALYSIS 2 (Summer 1976): 499-526.

The author argues that this country is presently trimming its objectives, because its social agencies have been asked to do more than they know how to accomplish. The schools receive a special lambasting for pretending that inputs are outputs and that they know what will work for their children. They are also described as an example of politicization without politics, with too great a federal influence upon their program planning. Corrections, crime control, and health are identified as other social policy areas in which intervention has had limited success. The author urges policy analysis to create the institutional structures and political arenas in which participants in the political process will be encouraged to support the agreements they make.

Wilkerson, C. David. "A Results-Oriented Development Plan." CONFERENCE BOARD RECORD 3 (March 1966): 40-45.

The article describes Kimberly-Clark's organization of an employee self-development program within an MBO planning context. The program's objectives were to maintain a high level of relevant professional and technical competence (continuously updated, expanded, and improved); to ensure that potential employees would see self-development opportunities within careers with the company; to help retain outstanding current employees; and to give current employees a more positive attitude toward the need for continuing their education.

Wisconsin. Division of Mental Hygiene. ADDENDUM: OVERVIEW OF GAS SCORE ANALYSIS AND PRACTICAL EXAMPLES. Madison: Division Program Evaluation and Research Section, April 1975. 32 p.

This report provides a full discussion of the division's view of the role that goal attainment scaling can play in program evaluation. Case studies illustrate scoring procedures for skills training for a variety of purposes, including toilet training.

Wynne, Edward. "Accountable to Whom?" SOCIETY 13 (January-February 1976): 30-37.

This article details the different interest groups to whom a school system might be accountable--parents, taxpayers, and intellectuals. The author contends that performance accountability measures should be studied within the context of the social values of the surrounding community. This is particularly true in the case of instruction for "moral conduct" and "good work habits," considered by many to be first priority functions of the schools.

Zody, Richard E. MANAGEMENT BY OBJECTIVES. Policy-Program Analysis and Evaluation Techniques. Package 6, Module 3. Washington, D.C.: National Training and Development Service, Urban Management Curriculum Development Project, n.d. 45 p.

A summary lecture outline is presented, emphasizing "important conditions for success." Also included are a "Goals for Gobbler" case study, and an essay summarizing public sector MBO literature by Kathleen A. Skaugen.

ADDENDUM

Altman, Stan. "Performance Monitoring Systems for Public Managers." PUB-
LIC ADMINISTRATION REVIEW 39 (January-February 1979): 31-35.

This is the fundamental argument for institutionalization of a management information system to monitor the performance of government in fulfilling its objectives. The author calls such an approach "the nervous system" for agencies which will detect problems in work processes impeding performance. He notes that
corrective actions may be incremental and may not unsettle
management-labor relations in the way that productivity programs
may do so.

Baldridge, J. Victor, and Tierney, Michael L. NEW APPROACHES TO MAN-
AGEMENT. San Francisco: Jossey-Bass, 1979. 220 p.

The authors review the experience of thirty-four institutions of
higher education which have adopted management by objective
and/or computerized management information systems. This study,
published by the Higher Education Research Institute, reports on
longitudinal data collected under an Exxon Education Foundation
grant. They report that these systems can reduce per student
expenditures, but may also encourage departmental competition.
Case studies are presented.

Bolan, Richard. "Community Decision Behavior: The Culture of Planning."
In A READER IN PLANNING THEORY, edited by Andreas Faludi, pp. 371-94.
Elmsford, N.Y.: Pergamon Press, 1973.

As a planner, the author sketches a model of the policymaking
environment surrounding planning. He defines four "variable sets":
process roles; decision field characteristics; planning and action
strategies; and issue attributes. He also details what the impact
of the public agenda may be upon decision outcomes, and plays
out the process steps involved in planning.

David, Elizabeth. "Benefit-Cost Analysis in State and Local Investment Decisions." PUBLIC ADMINISTRATION REVIEW 39 (January-February 1979): 23-26.

Addendum

The author argues that traditional benefits of the approach remain true on a state and local level. Information gaps are pointed up. Underlying criteria for the definition of need for the investment are called into question. Uniformity in measuring benefits of all projects considered in the investment package is to be ensured. Yet it may prove to be inappropriately expensive. Also, analysis may be distorted when local factor prices do not reflect relative scarcities, and when implementation may affect relative prices.

Elmore, Richard F. COMPLEXITY AND CONTROL: WHAT LEGISLATORS AND ADMINISTRATORS CAN DO ABOUT IMPLEMENTATION. Public Policy Paper, no. 11. Seattle: University of Washington Institute of Governmental Research, 1979. 45 p.

This paper features dialog between a legislative committee chairman and state education agency administrators. Two approaches to implementation are illustrated. A regulatory approach emphasizes heirarchical control and compliance, while a pragmatic approach may sacrifice some aspects of compliance to facilitate enhanced service delivery capacity via more delegated control.

_____. "Staffing the Mayor and Council: Analysis and Political Power in Seattle." WASHINGTON PUBLIC POLICY NOTES 8 (Winter 1980): 1-6.

This article details the history of the policy analysis institutional structure within Seattle city government. That city's Office of Policy Planning was initiated to foster comprehensive planning, but emerged also as the analytic staffing arm of the mayor's office. After five years, and changes in mayoral administrations, a good deal of this staff capability was shifted into line departments.

Herzlinger, Regina E. COST ACCOUNTING FOR WSFH. Boston: Intercollegiate Case Clearing House, 1977. Case 9-176-258. 7 p.

This case presents the problem of how to price the costs of local public television programming in order to solicit community underwriters willing to pick up those costs. Calculations need to be developed to establish the cost per hour of production.

Herlinger, Regina E., and Biteman, James H. UNIVERSITY HOSPITAL. Boston: Intercollegiate Case Clearing House, 1975. Case 9-176-020. 13 p. Teaching Note 4-176-204. 9 p.

This case is concerned with the double-distribution of overhead method of cost accounting. What would be the impact upon the hospital's finances if a group practice were to be organized for staff physicians? This issue emerged because of the perceived need to keep staff compensation competitive with private practice.

Kinsland, Dwaine; Wallace, William A.; and Axelrod, Donald. COST CONTROL IN THE MEDICAL ASSISTANCE PROGRAM: ONE STATE'S EXPERIENCE.

Boston: Intercollegiate Case Clearing House, 1975. Case 9-178-674. 25 p.
Teaching Note 5-178-675. 49 p.

The case presents discussions of the institutional framework surrounding Medicaid and the evolution of cost containment policies, in
order to enable readers to evaluate alternative options for produc-
ing short-term savings.

Meehan, Eugene J. THE QUALITY OF FEDERAL POLICYMAKING: PRO-
GRAMMED FAILURE IN PUBLIC HOUSING. Columbia: University of Missouri
Press, 1979. 230 p.

The author contributes a rich institutional history of implementation of the public housing program in St. Louis. He communicates
outrage at the agency's failure to learn what he views to be its
lessons, via extensive interpretation of data and the presentation
of sixteen pages of photographs of Pruitt-Igoe, and other loci of
its operations.

Meyer, Laurence H., and Rasche, Robert H. "On the Costs and Benefits of
Anti-Inflation Policies." FEDERAL RESERVE BANK OF ST. LOUIS REVIEW 62
(February 1980): 3-14.

This is an example of an analysis by economists of the inflation-
unemployment trade-offs problems. The costs of reducing inflation
are estimated under three models: an expectations-augumented
Phillips curve model; a monetarist model of the relationship of
monetary change to both inflation and unemployment; and a rational expectations mode. Ultimately, the authors have difficulty
in satisfactorily developing meaningful comparisons.

Montjoy, Robert S., and O'Toole, Laurence J., Jr. "Toward a Theory of
Policy Implementation: An Organizational Perspective." PUBLIC ADMINIS-
TRATION REVIEW 39 (September-October 1979): 465-76.

The authors examine case situations in which there are different
levels of resource availability and mandate specificity. They reviewed a sample of 191 U.S. General Accounting Office implementation reports, and compared combinations of the factors identified above against a four-part categorization system: (1) displacement toward goals, worldview; (2) new routines, new subunit,
start-up difficulties; (3) displacement toward existing routines; and
(4) resistance, backlogging, and refusal to implement.

Nakamura, Robert T., and Smallwood, Frank. THE POLITICS OF POLICY
IMPLEMENTATION. New York: St. Martin's Press, 1980. 201 p.

In a valuable succinct effort designed to define the policymaking
environment for public sector decisions, the authors lay out models
of three separate interrelated functional environments--policy formation, policy implementation, and policy evaluation (as well as the
special problems of judicial implementation). They examine the

political constraints and forces at work within each environment. They also trace the linkages between the three environments, and discuss the different roles leaders can play in helping to shape and guide implementation.

The authors also provide a summary review of earlier work on the subject by Donald S. Van Meter and Carl E. Van Horn, Milbrey McLaughlin, Eugene Bardach, Beryl Radin, and Martin Rein and Francine Rabinovitz.

Oxenfeldt, Alfred R. COST-BENEFIT ANALYSIS FOR EXECUTIVE DECISION MAKING. New York: AMACOM, 1979. 432 p.

Taking the position that economists and executives have basically different viewpoints and interests, the author nevertheless makes a case for the practical value of economic theory in those areas in which he finds there to be unreliability in plain common sense. In an accessible manner, employing cases framed as dialogs, he focuses upon the costs of executive decisions, the life cycle of a cost, the determinants of business benefits and the allocation of benefits to various parties in the business process, and the concept of "rival-related" decisions.

Radin, Beryl A. "The Implementation of SSI: Guaranteed Income or Welfare?" PUBLIC WELFARE 32 (Fall 1974): 7-19.

The article reports that, in the first year of conversion to the new Supplemental Security Income System, the legislative intent to develop a clean system of payments often became obscured. Welfare and income maintenance concepts have benefited from lessons learned in the conversion process. For example, if responsiveness to individual needs is to be viewed as desirable, supplementation policy must be developed. Determination of levels of payment is very complex, given other Social Security programs, as well as cost-of-living variations across the country.

Reed, Leonard. "The Joy of SES." WASHINGTON MONTHLY 12 (September 1980): 43-48.

Bonus awards in the Senior Executive Service often are awarded largely based upon the extent to which an administrator has flubbed, met, or exceeded his or her goals. An unimpressive example presented by the author was the filling of three vacant senior-level positions by a specific date--speedier action would have exceeded the goal.

Stone, Clarence. "The Implementation of Social Programs: Two Perspectives." JOURNAL OF SOCIAL ISSUES 36 (1980): 9-21.

The author places in perspective the managerial view that implementation is a technical process of achieving specified and agreed-

upon goals. He discusses how both economists and political so-
ciologists have addressed these matters. Goal modification, he
writes, is endemic to the process of moving from goal-setting to
concrete action. In his own view, implementation problems are
fundamentally political and require a political, not technical,
solution.

Urban Land Institute. REDUCING THE DEVELOPMENT COSTS OF HOUSING:
ACTIONS FOR STATE AND LOCAL GOVERNMENT. Proceedings of the HUD
National Conference on Housing Costs, 25-27 February 1979. Washington,
D.C.: U.S. Department of Housing and Urban Development, Office of Policy
Development and Research, 1979. 275 p.

Five papers were presented on the subjects of: zoning and design
standards for fringe communities; nine causes of land supply cost
problems, mechanisms for more easily securing title to underused
or abandoned inner-city properties, the allocation of development
costs between homebuyers and taxpayers, and procedural reform of
local land use regulation.

Wildavsky, Aaron. SPEAKING TRUTH TO POWER: THE ART AND CRAFT OF
POLICY ANALYSIS. Boston: Little, Brown and Co., 1979. 431 p.

A number of the essays in this volume are particularly relevant to
the consideration of decision-making processes. Chapter 2 reprints
the author's views on the "strategic retreat" on objectives. Chapter 7 is concerned with opportunity costs and merit wants. Chapter 5 presents the author's specific views on the analysis, politics,
and planning discussion, enabling him to comment on the problems
associated with rationality.

ADDRESSES OF ORGANIZATIONS
LISTED AS SOURCES,

Addiction Research Foundation
33 Russell Street
Toronto, Ont., Canada   M5S 2S1

American Bar Association
Correctional Economics Center
Suite 609
901 North Washington Street
Alexandria, Va.   22314

American Enterprise Institute for
   Public Policy Research
1150 Seventeenth Street, NW
Washington, D.C.   20036

Association of the Bar of the City
   of New York
42 West Forty-fourth Street
New York, N.Y.   10036

Boulder, Colorado
Office of the Budget Administrator
P.O. Box 791
Boulder, Colo.   80306

Brandeis University Florence Heller
   Graduate School for Advanced
   Studies in Social Welfare
Waltham, Mass.   02154

California, University of, Institute of
   Urban and Regional Development
Berkeley, Calif.   94704

California State Department of Health
Center for Health Statistics
744 P Street
Sacramento, Calif.   95814

Children's Defense Fund
1520 New Hampshire Avenue, NW
Washington, D.C.   20036

Citizens Educational Task Force
5101 McRee
St. Louis, Mo.   63110

City Almanac
Center for New York City Affairs
New School for Social Research
66 Fifth Avenue
New York, N.Y.   10011

Coalition for a National Health
   Service
P.O. Box 6586
T Street Station
Washington, D.C.   20009

Colorado, University of, Center for
   Management and Technical Programs
P.O. Box 3253
Boulder, Colo.   80303

Cornell University
Program on Science, Technology, and
   Society
Ithaca, N.Y.   14853

Crozer-Chester Medical Center
Community Mental Health Center
1439 Upland Avenue
Chester, Pa. 19103

Delaware State Department of Public
    Instruction (Public Information
    Office)
Dover, Del. 19901

Dellcrest Children's Centre
1645 Sheppard Avenue, W.
Downsview, Ont., Canada M3M 2X4

Denver, University of, Research
    Institute
2115 University Boulevard, S.
Denver, Colo. 80210

Denver Urban Observatory
University Center
Box A097
4200 Colorado Boulevard
Denver, Colo. 80220

District of Columbia Office of
    Budget and Financial Management
Room 411
District Building
Fourteenth and E Streets, NW
Washington, D.C. 20004

Duke University Institute of Policy
    Sciences
Duke Station 4875
Durham, N.C. 27706

Economic Development Council of the
    City of New York
230 Park Avenue
New York, N.Y. 10017

Educational Testing Service
Rosedale Road
Princeton, N.J. 08541

Fairview Heights, Illinois, City
    Government
City Hall
Fairview Heights, Ill. 62232

Florida State Department of
    Community Affairs
2571 Executive Center Circle, E.
Tallahassee, Fla. 32301

Georgetown University Public Services
    Laboratory
Washington, D.C. 20007

George Washington University
    State-Local Finances Project
Bookstore
2110 I Street, NW
Washington, D.C. 20037

Government Research Corporation
1730 M Street, NW
Washington, D.C. 20036

Harvard University Department of
    City and Regional Planning
Cambridge, Mass. 02138

Health Service Action. See Coalition
    for a National Health Service

Hospital Research and Educational
    Trust
840 North Lake Shore Drive
Chicago, Ill. 60611

Howard University Institute for Urban
    Affairs and Research
2401 Sixth Street, NW
Washington, D.C. 20059

Illinois Office of Education
State Board of Education
100 North First Street
Springfield, Ill. 62777

International Personnel Management
   Association
Suite 870
1850 K Street, NW
Washington, D.C.   20006

Ithaca, New York, City Government
City Hall
Ithaca, N.Y.   14850

Jewish Vocational Service Research
   Utilization Laboratory
1 South Franklin Street
Chicago, Ill.   60606

Joint Center for Urban Studies of the
   Massachusetts Institute of Technology
   and Harvard University
55 Wheeler Street
Cambridge, Mass.   02138

Lakewood, Colorado
Office of the City Administrator
44 Union Boulevard
Lakewood, Colo.   80228

League of California Cities
1108 O Street
Sacramento, Calif.   95814

Los Angeles County Chief
   Administrative Officer
713 Hall of Administration
Los Angeles, Calif.   90012

Medgar Evers College Institute of
   Public Administration
1127 Carroll Street
Brooklyn, N.Y.   11225

Michigan, University of, School of
   Social Work
Continuing Education Program in
   Human Services
1015 East Huron
Ann Arbor, Mich.   48109

MITRE
McLean, Va.   22101

Monsanto Corp.
8201 Idaho
Creve Coeur, Mo.   63111

National Municipal League
Carl H. Pforzheimer Building
47 East Sixty-eighth Street
New York, N.Y.   10021

National Planning Association
1606 New Hampshire Avenue, NW
Washington, D.C.   20009

National Training and Development
   Service for State and Local
   Government
5028 Wisconsin Avenue, NW
Washington, D.C.   20016

National Training and Information
   Center
1123 West Washington Boulevard
Chicago, Ill.   60607

New Jersey State Department of
   Community Affairs
P.O. Box 2768
363 West State Street
Trenton, N.J.   08625

New Jersey State Legislature
Office of Fiscal Affairs
Division of Program Analysis
Suite 232
State House
Trenton, N.J.   08625

New School for Social Research
Department of Urban Affairs and
   Policy Analysis
66 Fifth Avenue
New York, N.Y.   10011

New York City Budget Bureau
Municipal Building
New York, N.Y.   10003

New York City Commission on Human
   Rights
Government Employment Unit
52 Duane Street
New York, N.Y.   10007

New York City Planning Commission
2 Lafayette Street
New York, N.Y.   10003

New York State Division of Human
   Rights
Bureau of Program Planning and
   Affirmative Action
Administrative Office
270 Broadway
New York, N.Y.   10007

North Carolina, University of,
   Institute of Government
Chapel Hill, N.C.   27514

North Carolina, University of, School
   of Public Health
Chapel Hill, N.C.   27514

Pennsylvania State University College
   of Medicine
Department of Behavioral Science
Milton S. Hershey Medical Center
Hershey, Pa.   17033

Phoenix, Arizona
Management and Budget Department
251 West Washington
Phoenix, Ariz.   85003

Police Foundation
Suite 400
1909 K Street, NW
Washington, D.C.   20006

Program Evaluation Resource Center
501 Park Avenue, S.
Minneapolis, Minn.   55415

Public Citizen's Health Research Group
2000 P Street, NW
Washington, D.C.   20036

Rutgers University
Center for Urban Policy Research
New Brunswick, N.J.   08901

St. Louis University Center for Urban
   Programs
Community Residential Treatment
   Center Institute
221 North Grand
St. Louis, Mo.   63103

San Diego, California
Comprehensive Management Planning
   Program
City Administration Building
202 C Street
San Diego, Calif.   92101

Southern Illinois University at
   Edwardsville
Center for Urban and Environmental
   Research and Services
Edwardsville, Ill.   62026

Southern Illinois University at
   Edwardsville
Graduate Urban Studies Program
Box 32A
Edwardsville, Ill.   62026

Stanford Research Institute
333 Ravenswood
Menlo Park, Calif.   94025

United Bronx Parents
791 Prospect Avenue
Bronx, N.Y.   10451

United Nations Association of the
United States of America
300 East Forty-second Street
New York, N.Y. 10017

University Research Corporation
Model Cities Evaluation Institute
4301 Connecticut Avenue, NW
Washington, D.C. 20036

Urban Institute
2400 M Street, NW
Washington, D.C. 20037

VITA Treatment Center
696 East Broad Street
Columbus, Ohio 43215

Washington, University of
Institute of Governmental Research
3935 University Way, NE
Seattle, Wash. 98105

Washington University Center for
Educational Field Studies
Skinker and Lindell
St. Louis, Mo. 63105

Wisconsin, University of
Industrial Relations Research Institute
Madison, Wis. 53715

Wisconsin, University of
Institute for Research on Poverty
Madison, Wis. 53715

Wisconsin Division of Mental Hygiene
Program Evaluation and Research
Section
Room 515
1 West Wilson Street
Madison, Wis. 53703

AUTHOR INDEX

This index includes authors, editors, translators, and other contributors to works cited in the text. It is alphabetized letter by letter and numbers refer to page numbers.

Author Index

Berger, Peter L. 74
Berkley, George 48-49
Berman, Howard 59
Bernstein, Blanche 30
Berry, Ralph E., Jr. 31
Besen, Stanley 53
Binner, Paul R. 62
Bitter, James 91
Black, Max 4
Blair, Louis 8
Bledsoe, Ralph C. 91
Block, Michael K. 31
Bloom, Benjamin 130
Blum, Henrick L. 4
Blumrosen, Alfred 112
Blumrosen, Ruth 112
Bode, Edward L. 89
Bogosian, Theodore 49
Bogue, Ted 69
Bolin, David C. 92, 114
Bone, Larry Earl 92
Bonstedt, Theodor 96
Borus, Michael E. 49-50, 55
Brady, Rodney H. 92
Brawer, Allen 24
Breindel, Charles R. 17-18
Brennan, John P. 50
Briggs, Terrence 23
Brintnall, Joan 92
Brook, Robert H. 31
Brown, David S. 29, 93
Brown, William 100
Browning, Edgar 55-56
Bruce-Briggs, Barry 31-32
Brunson, John 90-91
Bullock, R.E.H. 106
Burchell, Robert W. 32
Burt, Marvin R. 4
Byassee, James 93

C

California. State Department of
    Health 93
Calsyn, Robert J. 93
Campbell, Vincent N. 93-94
Capron, William 53
Carlisle, Howard M. 139
Carlson, Georgina D. 94
Carnegie Council on Policy Studies
    in Higher Education 94, 136

Caro, Francis G. 15, 97-98
Caro, Robert 74
Carroll, Stephen J. 50, 94, 141
Cerish, Thomas K. 110
Children's Defense Fund of the
    Washington Research Project 15
Christenson, Charles 15-16, 50-51,
    87
Christenson, Tom H. 95
Churchill, Neil G. 95
Churchman, C. West 4
Ciarlo, James 95
Ciccinelli, Louis F. 95
Clark, Kenneth 100
Clark, Toni 90-91
Clavan, Sumner N. 137
Coates, Caroline 68
Coates, Joseph F. 5
Cobb, Roger 72, 74
Cody, Thomas 113
Cohen, David K. 125
Cohen, Jacob 100
Cohn, Edwin J. 51
Cole, Charles B. 48, 52
Cole, George F. 32
Collignon, Frederick C. 51
Conley, Ronald W. 51
Conover, C. Johnston 54
Correia, Eddie 32
Cotton, David L. 32-33
Cuban, Larry 74-75
Culliton, Barbara J. 33
Cunningham, James V. 75
Cuomo, Mario 75

D

Dahl, Robert A. 75, 82
Das, Amiya K. 33
David, Preston 16
David, Stephen M. 73-74
Davie, Bruce 48
Davies, J. Clarence III 75
Davies-Avery, Allyson 31
Davis, Howard 92, 96
Dean, Edwin 96
Deegan, Arthur V. 96
Delaware. State Department of
    Public Instruction 97
DeMont, Billie 97

Author Index

Author Index

Mack, Ruth Prince 5, 9
Mackay, John A.H. 120
MacKenzie, R. Alec 120-21
McKinsey and Company 20
Magee, John F. 10
Magoon, Albert J. 121
Mahler, Walter R. 121
Maiben, Dean 121
Maidlow, Spencer T. 59
Maize, Kennedy P. 122
Malck, Frederick 121-22
Manion, Patrick 20
Marco, Gary L. 101
Marcus, William B. 59
Marik, Robert H. 122
Marimont, Rosalind B. 122
Marmor, Theodore R. 38-39
Marriott, Richard H. 113
Marshall, Eliot 60, 132
Martin, Roscoe C. 80
Martuza, Victor R. 121
Mason, Edward G., Jr. 123
Massell, Adele P. 39
Massey, Hugh G. 39
Mates, William 49
Mathison, Mansel 107
Mauger, Paul 123
Maull, Perry J. 135
Max, Laurence 60
May, Rollo 114
Mechling, Jerry E. 10
Meltsner, Arnold 80
Mendelson, Robert 63, 78
Menges, Robert J. 120
Merelman, Richard M. 80
Merewitz, Leonard 39
Merton, Robert K. 80
Metsch, Jonathan M. 83
Meyer, Herbert H. 123-24
Meyerson, Martin 81
Michigan. Department of Education 124
Miller, Gary H. 131
Mirer, Thad 55
Mishan, Edward J. 60
Model Cities Evaluation Institute 124
Mohring, Herbert 5
Molander, C.F. 124
Monkman, Gail S. 36

Monsanto Co. 124
Moore, Mark 20
Morgan, Peter 69
Morrisey, George L. 125
Morse, Philip M. 5-6
Moscatello, Harry J. 21
Moses, Robert 74
Mosteller, Frederick 69
Mowitz, Robert J. 81
Muir, William K., Jr. 21
Munch, Patricia 60
Munger, Frank 80
Munson, Fred C. 35
Murphy, Jerome T. 125
Murphy, Richard T. 101
Murphy, Serre 21
Mushkin, Selma 10-11, 21-22
Muzzin, Linda 136
Myers, Sumner 5

N

Nader, Ralph 39
National Academy of Sciences. Institute of Medicine 61
Needles, Belverd, Jr. 39-40
Nelson, Carl W. 61
Nelson, Roxie 90-91
Neuhaus, Richard John 74
Newhouse, Joseph P. 40, 69
New Jersey. Office of Dispute Settlement 22
Newland, Chester 126
Newport, Lou 22
New York City. Department of City Planning 22
New York City. Mayor's Management Advisory Board 11, 127-28
New York State Moreland Act Commission on Nursing Homes and Residential Facilities 40
Nichols, Albert 69
Nichols, Daryl G. 93-94
Niedermeyer, Fred 128
Niskanen, William 53, 61, 81
Noble, John M., Jr. 61-62
Northrup, David E. 40
Norton, Eleanor Holmes 113
Norton, Steven D. 128
Novick, David 39

162

Author Index

TITLE INDEX

This index includes titles of books, articles, papers, dissertations, and reports cited in the text. It is alphabetized letter by letter and numbers refer to page numbers.

D

SUBJECT INDEX

This index is alphabetized letter by letter. Numbers refer to page numbers.

Subject Index

DATE DUE

DEMCO 38-297